I'M
LISTENING

Stuart M. Losen PhD

authorHOUSE®

AuthorHouse™
1663 Liberty Drive
Bloomington, IN 47403
www.authorhouse.com
Phone: 833-262-8899

Published by AuthorHouse 04/20/2022

ISBN: 978-1-6655-5761-0 (sc)
ISBN: 978-1-6655-5762-7 (e)

CONTENTS

Introduction.. vii

The Art of Listening.. 1
A Most Influential Professor... 7
A Magnificent Success..11
Like Kohler and the Apes...15
I Served Enough Time... 21
No Sneering Allowed 29
A Moment I'd Like to Forget 35
I Hate Shrinks.. 37
I'm Listening 45
A Hole in His Head 53
Our Worst Fear... 59
Just Like Mike.. 63
Back on Track 71
Memories 75
I've Got You Babe 79
Forgetfulness, Poor Hearing, and Sex..................................... 85
Call Me Raymond... 91
On Being an Expert Witness.. 97

Endnote: From the Author's Wife 107

INTRODUCTION

While compiling these accounts of my experiences as a psychologist, I realized that I had little idea about my intended audience other than my family, friends, and anyone else who might be interested. This book, therefore, is meant to be my legacy, a collection of memoirs describing events I experienced from the time I chose to pursue psychology as my life's work until I retired a little more than ten years ago. But what I didn't expect is how gratifying it has been to rewrite, and thereby relive, many of these past experiences, and to contemplate how they shaped my career.

The early accounts I've included, for example, focus upon certain childhood experiences which sensitized me toward becoming a good listener, followed by references to how impressed I was by two of my college professors regarding their work as psychologists. From that point on, I have included incidents which occurred during my internship, graduate school and assignment to Brooke Army Hospital immediately following the Korean War. The rest are descriptions of my work as a teacher, therapist and family-court expert witness.

I have changed all client names to safeguard their identity as well as the names of any institutions.

I hope you enjoy these accounts of my experience and find them of as much interest as I did re-living them.

Dedicated with love to Joyce, my LLW and editor,
to Laurie and Joe, Dan and Sarah,
to our grandsons, Sam and Lenny,
and our granddaughters Annie and Molly
and their significant others.

Special thanks to my coach, Jan Bassin
for her guidance and encouragement
and to the members of our Creative Writers Workshop at the
Westport Community Senior Center
for their helpful comments and suggestions.

Thanks also to Rhona Ceppos
for her ability to transform my scribbles and cross-outs
into legible manuscripts.

THE ART OF LISTENING

I grew up during the 1930's in an area of the East Bronx known as St. Raymond's Parish. St. Raymond's Church, and the nearly mile long stretch of open fields south of the church's cemetery, often gave travelers the impression of isolation from the rest of the Bronx when they trolleyed out to our area.

In my own neighborhood, mine was the only Jewish family, among a predominantly first generation Italian and Irish Catholic population. So, growing up, I was often picked on, called names, and bullied. I actually sensed threat whenever I walked past the row houses adjacent to our apartment building, and I had few friends, either at home or at school. I even had to learn street- fighting skills to defend myself, in order to gain a little respect--when running away was not an option. As a result, I felt very different from all the other kids, except for one, Alby, a few years older than me, but also often shunned or rejected. The other kids thought he was weird-- because he acted strange. He made funny noises, and, sometimes, he ran about impulsively, yelling and cursing unexpectedly in a way that, today, might be diagnosed as Tourette's syndrome. Anyway, Alby and I had a secret hideaway. It was our safe place, just under the train trestle over Bronxdale Avenue, across from St. Raymond's Church. We'd go there almost every day and spend hours listening to one another's problems, or we'd talk about how we might get even with the kids who gave us a hard time. Then we'd throw pebbles at the cars passing underneath the trestle, and we'd talk about what we wanted to be when we grew up. Alby said he wanted to become a priest, because he liked being an altar boy at St. Raymond's. And I said I wanted to become a prize- fighter like Joe Louis, who was then the heavyweight champion of the world.

Then, around 1940, the huge Parkchester housing development was built on the land where the open fields had been, and all those new apartment buildings began to attract a more diverse population. For me, new life-changing opportunities beckoned. For one thing, Parkchester had long, smooth beautifully paved roads to roller skate on, and the extravagant Loews American movie theater was where I got to meet a whole bunch of new kids. One of them invited me to join a new Boy Scout troop that met in a storefront on the other side of Parkchester. "It's the same storefront," he said, "where the synagogue meets."

I'd just turned twelve, the age you had to be to join the Boy Scouts of America, so I thought I'd give it a try.

I felt immediately welcomed and accepted. There were a few other Jewish kids in the troop and I found out that Mr. Michaels, the pudgy, round-faced Scoutmaster, was also Jewish.

Marching in uniform, with my new comrades in holiday parades, was exciting. Learning to tie different kinds of knots and outdoor camping skills was also a lot of fun. But most of all, I just loved palling around with my new troop- mates. There were no putdowns. I didn't get called names, and I didn't have to defend myself against any bullies. Scouting felt great! I took to it in a big way, advanced quickly through the ranks, and soon became a Patrol Leader. Mr. Michaels even praised me for my leadership skills. He actually congratulated me for "living up to all the qualities of a Good Scout." He said I exemplified courtesy, kindness, loyalty, cheerfulness, helpfulness, etc., etc.. Then he said that he was considering recommending me to the borough district office as our troop's nominee for the Boy Scout's honor society, the "Order of the Arrow".

I'd heard that the Order of the Arrow was a fraternity-like body within Scouting, which was known for its high status among Scouts all over the world. Members of the Arrow had secret handshakes. They also had secret words when they greeted one another, and they wore long white sashes on their uniforms when they marched in parades.

But then, Mr. Michaels cautioned that I might be competing against one or two other boys in our troop who were also being considered for the honor of being our troop's nominee, and that there would be an election in a few months to see who got the majority of the votes of all the troop members. Final induction into the Order of the Arrow, he added, would then take place, during a borough-wide "Indian style" tapping ceremony, held during the summer at the area's Boy Scout "ten-mile river" camp in upstate New York.

I was excited. My parents reveled in my having "become such a big success." They said that from all the nice things they'd heard from Mr. Michaels about me, they were certain I would be voted into the Arrow.

But I wasn't so sure. I knew I could count on the support of all of the kids in my Patrol. But there were three other Patrols in the troop. I didn't know how popular I might be among them. They didn't know me. And I didn't know if there actually would be other nominees to the Arrow from our troop with whom I might be competing. That worried me. There were two months to go before the election was held, and I didn't know what I could do to assure that I'd be chosen. I felt that if I didn't win the election, it would be a big disappointment, like a failure really, and as a kind of rejection by others like that which I'd experienced only too often back in my old neighborhood.

So I chose to do things I later came to regret. I spent a lot of time during troop meetings trying to ingratiate myself, trying to get kids, especially those in the other patrols, to like me enough to want to vote me into the Arrow. I went out of my way to be attentive, to carefully listen to what other kids had to say, to help them with their knot tying, or their studying for merit badges, whatever. I also volunteered to help Mr. Michaels with any tasks he and/or his assistants might have for me, and I told the other Patrol Leaders that I would make myself available to help any of their kids with any special projects they might have. Again, I listened a lot to everyone. I smiled a lot! And it came easy!

But then I began questioning what I was doing. I wasn't really doing things, listening very carefully, or helping others to really like me-- for me. What I began to regret was the growing feeling that I was being dishonest, that I was manipulating others just so they would vote me into the Arrow. I was being insincere. I was simply being phony, and I also didn't like how that came so easily.

Back in my old neighborhood, it seemed to me that I had always been a good listener, that when the kids my age and older gave me a hard time or outright rejected me, I found comfort joining the younger kids in their street games. They always deferred to me, asked for my advice when they had problems, and they considered me their "Protector" when I helped them ward off being bullied by any of the older kids – the ones I could handle.

I'd also been able to hear- out one or two of the older girls on our street who complained about their macho- brothers who'd always put them down and made them feel miserable. One of them, in fact, who said my advice had helped her, started calling me "the Professor." I liked that.

All of that, I felt, was part of who I was. I felt accepted, appreciated for being helpful to others, who like me, had experienced difficulties, if not outright rejection, in their relationships with others.

So, with my troop- mates, during my tour of duty in the Boy Scouts of America, I had once again demonstrated being a good listener, and the best helper anyone could ask for. But my renewed efforts were almost entirely intended to garner votes for election to the Order of the Arrow. I felt like I'd simply become a manipulator. In a way, I felt accomplished, like I could be good at it when I needed to, but I was troubled over feeling I chose to do all that just to win some votes.

Anyway when time came for the big election, I won hands down! The vote for me was unanimous. Also, as it turned out, there were no other contenders for the nomination. And, finally, at summer camp during the big "tapping" ceremony, I was the first of all the borough finalists inducted into the Order of the Arrow. That, of course, made me, my parents, Mr. Michaels and our whole troop all very proud.

Looking back over the many years since my Boy Scout experience, though still proud I made the Arrow, I also remember, with regret, what I felt I had to do to win that prize. What I learned, therefore, at age 14, was that being phony was costly. It affected how I viewed myself. My listening skills, honed by difficult times during those earlier years, eventually did prove valuable regarding the work I did in connection with my choice of profession. But, I also learned to stay away from politics.

A MOST INFLUENTIAL
PROFESSOR

He walked into the classroom seemingly oblivious to us students already assembled. With shoulders hunched forward he shuffled toward the podium and slid his weathered brown leather briefcase behind the lectern after first removing a dog-eared folder of lecture notes. He appeared unaware of us seated in the front row, waiting expectantly, like hungry chicks waiting for a worm, or any new idea he might utter. Still with his back to us, Dr. Goldstein removed his woolen cap, glanced briefly at a small tear in its lining and then placed it and his frayed scarf on a chair behind the lectern. He took off his loosely fitting overcoat, placed it, too, on the chair and finally turned to face us.

"Does he seem out of it?" a classmate whispered.

"Shh". I nudged him." Give him a chance. He's almost eighty."

"This evening." He began softly. We…"

"Would you please speak louder, Dr. Goldstein," someone called out.

"This evening—you can hear me? — Gut!" he fumbled with a page of notes.

"We will talk about the gradual evolution of the brain development of the or—gan—ism." With his very perceptible German accent he drew out the word organism for special emphasis. "We will come to understand the concept of 'self-actualization.' It is the way the organism comes to behave, as good as humans can, to realize our full potential."

Goldstein lectured for several minutes about his study of evolving

7

changes in human brain capacity since the days of the caveman. He was enroute to explaining what he later described as *the gradual emergence of our modern capacity for categorical thinking,* or what he termed *man's unique capacity for the abstract attitude.* Bur just *before* he arrived at his concluding statements, his voice increasingly strident, confident that he would impress us, his rapt students, with findings from his many years of extensive neuro-psychological research, he was suddenly interrupted.

"But Dr. Goldstein, Dr. Goldstein, --" an annoyingly obtrusive voice from the back of the room --probably the same student who had asked him to speak louder.

"If what you've said so far is true," his interrupter persisted, sounding more like a prosecutor in criminal court, "*how then* do *you* account for the Neanderthal Man?" It was really more an accusation than a question.

Stepping forward, Goldstein paused thoughtfully and ran his hand through his wispy gray hair. He stared for a minute at the student waiting expectantly for an answer. A smile crossed his face.

"Well," he said with a shrug," I never met him." Then he stepped back behind the podium to resume his lecture.

Kurt Goldstein, along with the famous educator John Dewey, was among the originators of the so-called *positivist school* of thinking regarding human nature, personality development and learning theory. They criticized Freud's essentially negative view of basic human nature and proposed instead that human beings usually behaved in ways primarily intended to more fully actualize or enhance themselves. Goldstein's view, which most impressed many of his Freudian-trained students, was a refreshing departure from the ego-defense psychology popular in the 1930's and 40's, and preceded Carl Rogers's influence among psychotherapists.

Goldstein the teacher was also an extraordinary model of professional excellence, which invited his students' emulation. He encouraged us to challenge his ideas, and though occasionally irked by an overbearing critic, his response was most often considerate and informative. He'd been irritated by the student who had interrupted his lecture and inappropriately insisted that he explain the applicability of his theory to Neanderthal Man, but Goldstein used humor to momentarily defuse his critic. He agreed later to meet with the student to discuss the issue further, but meanwhile he had deftly avoided a potentially disruptive incident in class.

Goldstein also invited student concern for his well-being because he seemed so vulnerable. He made light of his being old and forgetful, but he nevertheless conveyed the impression that helping the absent-minded professor might sometimes be necessary. Once, in fact, Dr. Goldstein was spotted waiting for a bus at a stop just off the main City College campus. It was snowing and bitterly cold; his unbuttoned overcoat had flared open while he feebly struggled with an uncooperative scarf to protect his face and neck. The student who had seen his plight ran over to help. "Here, Dr. Goldstein, let me give you a hand, "he said. "You seem to be having some trouble."

"Ach, viele danken" muttered Goldstein. "My scarf it will not cooperate." He then thanked the student several times until his bus came into view. Then he waved his appreciation to the rest of us, who had come over to make sure he boarded safely. The following week, Dr. Goldstein referred to the help he'd received at the bus stop as an example of man's inherent willingness to help others in need. One of the few Black students in our class answered wryly.

"Depends if you're the right color."

"And the Nazis," said another, "how do you figure them?"

Dr. Goldstein looked sadly down at his notes and shook his head. "Such things are really not hard to understand," he said. "It is unfortunate. Such behavior is not normal, such destructive behavior, --but inside, those people have been trained to believe they are doing the right thing—that it is justified. That is how they are taught."

"And crazy people?" someone asked. "How does insane behavior enhance a schizophrenic's inner self, or his well-being, or his survival?"

Goldstein smiled and looked around the class. "Our schizophrenic has withdrawn from the world because everything has become so painful. His paranoia, his behavior which we call dissociative, his words-- make no sense. It is his way of keeping from feeling more pain. He cannot cope with the real world, so he hides inside a world he makes up for himself. When that doesn't work, he withdraws a little more or he becomes what we call catatonic. You understand?"

What Goldstein described to account for unacceptable, inappropriate and pathological, as well as racist, anti-social behavior had a profound influence on many of us students like myself, who went on to work in mental health fields, He helped us to view aberrant behavior not as just crazy or non-sensical, but as behavior we needed to more closely listen to, and examine like a detective examining the clues at a crime scene to determine its sometimes hidden meaning. That included identifying the perception of purpose which compelled someone to act "crazy."

Today, after many years of experience in working with people whose behavior is difficult to understand, and who resist change even though they have come for help, I often think back fondly and appreciatively to our absent-minded professor who couldn't keep his scarf in place while waiting for a bus on a cold, wintry night.

A MAGNIFICENT SUCCESS

We had no idea that our instructor, a Black man, a newly appointed assistant professor in his mid-thirties, would soon play an important role in the 1954 Supreme Court decision known as "Brown vs. the Bd. of Ed." None of us then, the 15 of us taking his Social Psychology class at CCNY, had any expectation that Dr. Clark's "doll studies", which he'd described to us, would provide the telling evidence about the feelings of inferiority experienced by Black children attending segregated schools in the "Jim Crow" south. It was Dr. Clark's findings, which Thurgood Marshall cited, while arguing their case before the United States Supreme Court, that convinced the Court that separate schools for Blacks and whites did not, and could not, result in a truly "equal" education for both. We also could not have known that, despite his significant role in bringing about the Court's 1954 desegregation decision, Dr. Clark would remain pessimistic for the rest of his life in his view-- that both the Brown decision and all the subsequent years of integration efforts would prove only minimally effective in reducing persistent racism.

During our seminars with Dr. Clark, he often paced back and forth, or sat dejectedly on the corner of his desk, chain-smoking, often staring down at the floor, quietly describing his studies. He'd become increasingly agitated as he described how so many children he'd interviewed felt poorly about themselves. They clearly believed that they were in no way the equal of those other children, those white children who lived across the tracks under more privileged circumstances. Dr. Clark didn't express any anger, as we might have expected. Instead, he said he felt a sense of despair about those children, who so early in their lives had already begun to adopt the prevailing view of white society that "colored" children weren't really worth educating.

Dr. Clark seemed so disheartened that he aroused our efforts to try to convince him otherwise. We would argue with him that the data he was accumulating would ultimately *have* to impress "important" others, that his findings could not be denied. We told him that he ought to take heart and not get so discouraged during the preliminary hearings he was then involved in, in the Virginia Commonwealth Courts. But Dr. Clark waved us off. He'd just quietly lean forward, puff a few more times on his cigarette, take us in with a sideways glance, and then gaze off toward the back of the room. "I really don't have much hope," he would say. "There's just too much against us – but I guess we'll just have to keep on going."

Dr. Clark frequently intimated that whatever successes he was currently experiencing in the courts would most likely be later reversed or overturned. Eventually, our persistent efforts to reassure him that he would ultimately help bring down segregation seemed to give him some comfort. But, apart from whatever small encouragement we may have provided, his persistent pessimism had a profound effect on all of us.

What we learned through our involvement in what Dr. Clark was experiencing raised everyone's awareness about civil rights. We were deeply affected. We saw the ugliness of racism through his eyes. We not only identified with his struggles, we empathized with his despair. It was as if he had inhaled each of us into his view of how insidious and destructive the forces of bigotry affected children's lives in segregated schools.

At that time, we were, of course, a select audience, very ready to learn from Dr. Clark's experiences. Back then, in the early 1950's, each of us was exploring the new field of psychology, a course of study about which few of us were familiar, and which wasn't at all the popular field it eventually became. Certainly, student interest in social psychology was even less evident then. Group-dynamics theory and problem-solving research, which evolved a decade or so later, had not yet had much impact. So when Kenneth Clark stimulated our interest in his research, and was able to arouse our concerns about segregation and racism through the report of his research findings, that in itself might be considered an accomplishment. We learned a lot from his description of the research difficulties with which he'd had to contend while working in segregated schools. We followed his weekly accounts of the legal battles he faced, reporting his findings to often disinterested if not openly hostile audiences. He drew us into his world and how he felt about his work in a very personal way; it was as if we took part in his ongoing courtroom battles which he'd described to us in great detail. I think, therefore, that perhaps without deliberately intending it, Dr. Clark made us feel that we had a considerable stake in the outcome.

A few years later, very much involved in my psychological studies, I completed an honors research project under Dr. Clark's supervision. We were studying attitude change among white City College students toward Negroes as a function of their campus interaction. The results were not very important, but what I learned from him about studying attitude change, especially about using then popular interview techniques, was invaluable. He emphasized two ideas. First, that attitude change stemming from everyday interracial experience was likely to be fleeting at best. More than likely, he asserted, such experience might only reinforce previously held stereotypical thinking, <u>unless</u> the new experience was intense and very positive, like playing together on a winning basketball team. Secondly, he was very critical of using multiple- choice questionnaire techniques to assess people's attitudes in general. He argued that those techniques were likely to produce extremely superficial data. He emphasized that <u>unless</u> subjects, being polled about their views, were also given some opportunity to elaborate upon what they'd said, the data would most likely reflect previously learned attitudes more than anything they'd learned from any new experience. Finally, he stressed the fact that racial attitudes are formed much earlier in childhood than I'd expected, and that such attitudes probably were related to attitudes formed regarding "difference" in general. He said that it takes a much greater accumulation of more recent experience with others, who had earlier been perceived as different, before anyone might overcome reinforced, frequently parentally-imbued attitudes.

Much of what I learned from Dr. Clark about racism and attitude change is generally better understood today. Attitude studies prior to the early 50's, were primarily linked to evaluations of traits of personality such as those used in "Authoritarian Personality" studies or "social distance" scales. Social psychological research is far more sophisticated today thanks to the teachings of people like Kenneth Clark. But what still stands out most in my memory of him, is how he evoked empathy and compassion in his students during those turbulent years which led up to the Supreme Court's decision that, regarding children's education, "Separate was not equal!"

Sadly, during his last years, Kenneth Clark was described as having perceived all of his accomplishments as a series of "magnificent failures." During the late 1970's he was also recorded as saying that he was even "more pessimistic" than he had been earlier. Certainly his "anguished" efforts produced much less positive change than he had hoped for. But some progress was made, even though many Civil Rights leaders currently perceive a marked trend backward toward de- facto segregationist policies and practices in our schools. Therefore, Dr. Clark's legacy may better be characterized by the tremendous impact his efforts have had upon our awareness of what still needs to be done. In one of his last publications, Dr. Clark stated that many whites in our society still do not recognize that their own self-interest may best be served by Black success. Because people of color may eventually become the majority in our changing "polyglot" nations, he asked "won't everyone see that it is to their advantage that Blacks succeed?" I became convinced about the wisdom of that view many years ago when I had the good fortune to study with him, and to learn, from his experience, that to believe otherwise is ultimately self-destructive. Hopefully, the ability he showed to touch others' lives will eventually come to be viewed as his "magnificent success" more than he might ever have thought he might achieve.

LIKE KOHLER AND
THE APES

Early in the spring of 1957, word came down that Dr. Gilbride, Chairperson of the Psychology Department at the University of Buffalo, wanted to see Steve and me as soon as possible. We had no idea why. Steve even said he thought we might be in trouble about having complained that the guest speaker at our last department meeting had put us to sleep. It was a boring talk about the mating behavior of tsetse flies, a topic, Steve had said, might have been fun to discuss, had the speaker not chosen to focus on experimental design.

Terry Gilbride ushered us into her office. The frown in her voice seemed unmistakable. She was obviously annoyed about something. Steve and I exchanged apprehensive glances, but said nothing.

"I've got a special teaching assignment for you gentlemen," she began. There was a note of sarcasm in her voice. "It is indeed a challenge, one our department has been asked to undertake for the sake of the college."

Steve and I looked at each other questioningly. I was about to ask TG (which was how we graduate students often referred to her) what she was talking about, when she started to laugh.

"Seriously," she said, waving off the air of momentousness created by her opening statement, "I hope you guys know a lot about football, or more, really, about football players - because I need you to teach two sections of Intro- Psych to our newly recruited football team."

"You're kidding!" I stammered.

"No way!" blurted Steve.

"Hold on, guys," Dr. Gilbride countered. "It's no big deal, really – calm down. You each will be assigned a freshman class of twenty or so of our football athletes, deemed particularly by our alumni, to be the financial hope and future of this academic institution. It is imperative, I am told, that these young stalwarts must meet minimal academic standards to remain eligible as students in good standing – so that they can bring fame and glory to our institution – and, thereby, stimulate more of the alumni contributions we evidently need to survive. You get it?"

"Yeah," I muttered, "I get it."

Steve was less enthusiastic.

"How are we supposed to teach these guys? Asked Steve. "They're impossible. They're remedial students, most of them. They can barely read their playbooks, let alone our intro texts. How are we supposed to get them through without being totally dishonest about what they need to accomplish?"

"It won't be easy," Gilbride answered. "But if anyone can reach them, you two can do the job. I know this is only your second year here, but I've heard about how good you are with our Intro classes. And you will get all the help you may need; modified texts, special workbooks, allocations for special tutoring – the whole, 9, or is it 10 yards – whatever you need. The eyes of Academia are upon you!" Then she added, with a dismissive wave of her hand and a big smile,

"Now get out of here – you can do it!"

I had no idea what to expect. I also had mixed feelings about working with our U.B. footballers. I had been an athlete in college, and I was an ardent N.Y.Giants football fan, but having to teach football players just to keep them eligible to stay in school—that was something else. Then, when they came to class for the first time, I was amazed at how big they were, their muscles bulging out of every sleeve or shirt opening. They filed into class like they were coming into a huddle, in groups of two or three, hunkering down in their seats, which were no match for their size. They sat quietly in the semi-circle I'd arranged for them, as if awaiting my play call. I hesitated at first, not sure how to start but then, on sudden impulse, I announced that I was "Coach Losen" and that "I'm here to get you through this course on Introduction to Psychology as best as I can." When they all laughed, I felt like I'd connected.

"Yo Coach," asked the biggest of them all, "do we really gotta come to all these classes? I mean, can't we get some kinda pass or something if we just show for a few and skip the rest? You know we gotta do a lot of extra training this spring to stay in shape – so can we …"

I cut him off. "No way," I said. I told them that the Academic Standards Committee required regular attendance at all classes, that the rules were strict, and that if they missed a class for any reason, it had to be made up by a tutoring session. "Ask your coach on that", I said." I think he'll back me up on no bending of the rules." Then I said, "Anyway -- some of the stuff we're going to cover might seem a little dry, but—" I paused," you may actually find a lot that's worth knowing about."

"Whaddaya mean dry?" asked someone in the second row. I couldn't see him at first, blocked by the two huge linemen sitting in front of him.

I explained that they might not get very excited by some of the subject matter we'd cover, like experimental statistics, or the studies of animal behavior outlined in their workbook, "but you may get something out of the stuff on different personalities and abnormal human behavior – might even help you in football."

"Oh yeah – how?" asked another mountain of a man sitting just to my right. He was so immense, he took up the space of two seats and totally obscured the man sitting behind him. I felt relieved to see that he was smiling as he asked his question.

"Check this out with your coach," I said. "I think you know it pays to learn as much as you can about anyone you're going to play. You study lots of charts about formations and how all those x's and o's are supposed to move, right? But don't you also study films, when you can get them, of the previous performance of players on the teams you face, before you actually get to play them? So you know it's helpful to get as much info as you can about your opponents – their style of play, how they respond to getting hit, what quirky mannerisms they may show that tip you off about their moves, their timing, etc. It's all part of your preparation right? Well, knowing about peoples' behavior, what turns them on or off and why – that's what a lot of this course is all about, you with me?"

"Yeah, okay – makes sense, Coach," said my amiable giant. But then he smirked, "What's the scoop about the text and the workbooks? We really gotta use them?"

"Yes," I answered. "The text for the course is one of the best I could find for you. It should be clear and easy to read. The workbook is even better, it summarizes all the main ideas covered in the text and has loads of diagrams to make things even clearer: You know from diagrams right? – so I'm sure you'll find them very helpful. Any more questions?"

There were a lot of questions, but mostly questions of the routine kind I would have expected from any new class of students, e.g.' about the number of quizzes, the final exam, tutoring availability, and did I have a favorite NFL team. I felt we had connected and I walked away from our first class feeling less apprehensive about how it might all work out. When I talked with Steve later that day, he described a similar experience, but he seemed less optimistic.

"I get the feeling it's gonna be a struggle to hold their interest, "he said. "Like their heads will still be out on the football field most of the time no matter how well I motivate or entertain them. You know, I even made a few jokes while we went through the orientation stuff."

"What happened?" I asked.

"No one laughed," said Steve. "They took notes."

After the next one or two sessions, I began feeling doubtful again. Steve was right about not being able to keep our football players focused. I studied the textbook to see what might be of greatest interest to them. Then I lectured about whatever I felt they absolutely needed to know, in the most novel ways I could think of—just to hold their interest. On one occasion, I even climbed up on my desk and imitated one of Kohler's apes, acting out the classic research findings which Dr. Kohler had recorded, of how the higher-order monkeys are capable of showing "insight." My students laughed hysterically at my apish fumbling with two sticks in order to obtain the banana situated just outside my cage. But they got the point, and one of them pounded me on my back afterward as they were leaving class.

"Hey that was something, Coach," he said. "I betcha those apes could even learn how to play football."

Steve, it turned out, also had an interesting experience dealing with his students' distractibility. He had been describing how rats learned to quickly navigate a maze when rewarded with cheese for making the best route choices. But when he saw that fewer and fewer of his students were paying attention and particularly when he spotted one of them reading his playbook, Steve said "that's when I lost it". I stopped lecturing. I told them to get out their workbooks and turn to the page that showed a diagram of the rat maze I had been describing. Then I handed out boxes of crayons while I told them to find the picture of the rat at the entrance to the maze and the cheese located in the goal box. 'See the alternate routes the rats can run to the goal-box to get the cheese?" I said, "See those routes? They're like the routes you run when you're going out for a pass. See them? – 'OK,- -now, color them in!'"

"What did you say?" I gasped. It was something I never would have done.

"I told them to color in the maze routes! That's what I said. I was so goddamned frustrated," Steve said." I told them to color the routes!"

"Wow," I said, "What did they do?"

"That's the best part," said Steve. "A couple of them got pissed. I could see them get all red-faced. But they did it. They colored the fucking maze-routes, tore the pages out of the workbooks and handed them to me as they left the room. One of them, in fact, had this big silly grin on his face. 'Good move man' he said. 'Six points for that one!'"

By the end of the semester, it was evident that Steve and I had, each in our own way, managed to get our football team through Introductory Psychology. We lost only one or two of them to academic ineligibility, but overall, we had a better track record than any other instructors who taught the courses they were required to take. Then, after final-exam week, Dr. Gilbride called us into her office to congratulate us on our success.

"I don't know how you two managed to do it," she said, smiling broadly, "but you got them through. Some of those kids have actually been asking for the two of you for next term. You know, If there were some kind of medal the college could reward you with, you'd get it."

Steve and I glanced at each other. Without missing a beat, we answered, "How 'bout the Purple Heart?"

I SERVED ENOUGH TIME

"These are my favorites, my babies," said Dr. Winters while he alternately hugged each of the two middle-aged men seated next to him. He had an arm around each one and kept drawing them closer to him as he talked. I stared in disbelief as he then chucked each of them under the chin while introducing them to me. "This is Charlie. He's a little slow." Dr. Winters winked at me. "And this one is Martin. He's our quiet one. They've been with me here on the ward for a few years now, haven't you boys?" Then Dr. Winters laughed. "They're good boys." He was beaming. "And this is their home." I nodded my acknowledgement of Dr. Winters' introduction and backed away. The whole scene made me feel nauseous.

That was my first day on the locked ward. It was the summer of 1957 and I was completing my required hospital residence tour of duty at Katonah VA Hospital. Winters was the Chief Psychiatrist on the unit, and had run the closed ward for more than twenty years. The twenty-five or so patients who daily roamed the halls and the day room, where I'd been introduced to Charlie and Martin, were among the most disturbed, neurologically impaired, and poorly functioning inmates found anywhere in America's VA hospitals. Surprisingly, at least to me, practically all of the patients on the ward were quiet, seemingly oblivious to one another, sometimes staring at nothing, frequently seated, or leaning against the hallway wall in fetal position. Some might be seen gesturing, mouthing or mumbling incoherently, and a few seemed rigidly transfixed – not moving at all. Occasionally one might shout something angrily, or curse at a nurse, or me passing by. But if a patient suddenly moved toward or motioned angrily at another patient, he would be quickly subdued by one or more of the aides who routinely patrolled the ward. That was rare. Uncontrollable, acting-out behavior was rarely seen on the ward. Most of the patients were long-term so-called "burned out" schizophrenics. A few of the older patients were brain-damaged veterans of World War II, and there were some younger Korean vets who had been recently admitted. Many previously "acting out" patients had been "quieted" by shock treatments or psychosurgery; consequently, few ever displayed the kind of agitated, wild-eyed destructive behavior one might expect to see on a psychiatric "back" ward.

On that first day when I came onto his ward, Dr. Winters assigned me to work primarily with a few Korean Vets. Later he told me that because I was young and had worked at Fort Sam with some of the brainwashed kids from the Korean POW camps, that I might have a better chance getting somewhere with them than some of the old-timers.

I spent a lot of time working with David, a 27 year old young man who had spent almost a year in a POW camp. He'd been captured in 1952 and was worked over by the Red Chinese during the year before the Korean "Police Action" ended. He'd walked up to me when I came on the ward one morning and told me in a soft, barely audible voice, that he was losing his brains every time he defecated. Then he hesitatingly held out a piece of toilet tissue for me to examine as proof that the gray streaks, barely discernible within the smears he pointed to, were brain cells. "There, see those streaks?" he whispered. "Brain cells are gray, aren't they?"

David insisted that he was losing more and more of his brain cells every day. "You gotta do something about this Doc," he said, his voice rising. "I'm losing my brains!"

I initially recoiled, but quickly regained my composure, and told him I was really upset for him if that was what was actually happening. However, I told him that I seriously doubted that he was actually losing his brains, despite what he was showing me. Anyway, I promised that I would arrange for a laboratory study of his feces just to make sure. I told him to leave his sample with the ward nurse and that I would tell him the results of the lab's analysis as soon as we got the report back. I left him standing there staring down at the tissue paper in his hand. He kept repeating, "I'm losing my fuckin' brains!"

I got Dr. Winters to approve what I wanted to try, and cued the ward nurse into my plan.

Two days later I sought David out in the day room.

"I've got good news, David," I said. "The lab report came back negative! They said that they found absolutely no trace of any brain tissue. Here, read it for yourself." I handed him an official looking diagnostic report that I'd prepared.

"Are you sure?" asked David. He almost looked saddened by the report.

"No trace, David – nothing," I repeated. David backed away, and turned to go.

"Wait David," I said. "I'm still concerned about this. What made you think you were losing your brains; when did that start? Can you tell me?"

David hesitated, but then sat down with me at a table in the dayroom. He began to speak slowly, hesitatingly.

"Can I trust you?"

"I had the lab workup done for you, didn't i?"

"You coulda had it faked."

"That's true, but I chose to take seriously what you told me about losing your brains – enough to try to check it out for you, but I can appreciate you not trusting me – why should you?"

"You're right – you can't trust anyone around here. I learned that in Korea – always watch your rear!"

Then David told me he thought maybe I could be trusted – from having seen me talking to other patients on ward rounds.

"They said you're different from Winters. He's a horse's ass! They said at least you listen to them."

"Okay, so I'm listening. What are you afraid of David?"

"I'm afraid of losing my brains. You already know that."

"Yeah, but if you're not, you've got nothing to worry about. The brain eventually compensates, at least partly, for anything you've lost"

"I thought brain cells can't regenerate."

"They don't. Other parts of the brain take over some lost functions. Parts that weren't much used before. It's only when you're much older that you don't regain lost functioning too well. Sounds like you've studied up on how the brain works. Have you?"

"A little – when I came back from Korea."

"So what's really scaring you, David?" I persisted.

"How do you know I'm scared, Doc? You know, apart from losing my brains?"

"Everyone here is scared – of something, of somebody – Everybody."

"So who are you scared of Doc?"

"Winters – the staff supervisors – the people who run the VA – we all have people who control some of what we're doing, or trying to do. What about you David?"

David studied me for a few seconds before he answered. "My CO. The captain in charge of my returning unit at Fort Dix just before I was discharged. I still think about him. He said I was a goddamned turn-coat and I ought to be dishonorably discharged or getting a Section Eight. He told me that all the medical attention I was getting at the clinic was a waste of taxpayers' money, and that all of us being treated there after we'd been brainwashed were worthless garbage. He said we all ought to be court-martialed. He wasn't kidding."

I nodded. "David, he was off base. He was probably some ignorant RA unit commander who didn't understand what you guys were put through when you were captured. We're still learning about what the Chinese did to you guys in the POW camps."

"Well, he said he didn't believe any of that crap about us being brainwashed. He said we were a bunch of sorry-assed cowards, yellower than the gooks. He cursed us out morning, noon and night. Said we were lower than snakes' bellies. He really chewed us out."

"How long was he actually in charge of you?"

"Just a couple of weeks – we were discharged pretty quick. Before Dix, they had already rehabbed us for over two months in Texas at Ft. Sam when we came back stateside. Then we were shipped up to Dix, me and about four or five others, for treatment and routine discharge. We'd been warned we might catch shit from the RA boys, but coming from that Captain – day in and day out for two whole weeks – that was hard to take – it made all of us crazy – it was like some of the shit that happened in the POW camps all over again."

Having been stationed at Fort Sam Houston, in San Antonio, Texas right after the Korean War ended, I had worked with some of our returning POWs who'd been brainwashed in Korea. The process was insidious and

24

inhumane. It had been developed by the Chinese communists to get captured GIs to sign documents and make anti-American radio broadcasts which were then used to try to influence the end of war negotiations at Panmunjom. The POWs selected for "brainwashing" were frequently isolated, and encouraged to believe that they'd been betrayed by the other inmates. They were also sleep-deprived. Their mail was clearly tampered with to make them feel they'd been abandoned by their friends and families and they were told that everyone back home considered them to be traitors. In other words, they were bullied, belittled, and then, after a while, when they were exhausted and demoralized, they began to get some relief, a few privileges at first, then more privileges and more little comforts, if they signed a few statements – innocent commentaries at first which were easy for them to agree to. But then, they were asked to sign documents that were increasingly more like confessions about atrocities, or horrible misdeeds which had been inflicted upon North Korean victims. It was a cleverly developed and devilishly elaborate method. It was used particularly with POWs who were not above NCO grade, who their captors felt might be easily manipulated into serving propaganda purposes. It was effective with many of our less-than-strong-willed servicemen. Unfortunately, the Fort Dix captain, in charge of David's group of dischargees, simply had ignored the efforts the Fort Sam psychologists had employed to get David and other brainwashed POWs feeling okay about themselves again. As a result, within a year of his discharge, David was admitted to a VA hospital for further psychiatric treatment. Now, two years later, he was still in bad shape.

David and I met and talked for a while each day after he'd described all that happened to him since his POW days. He described in detail how, following his discharge, he returned home to his family who initially were supportive. But then they grew impatient with his moodiness and general malaise. They began telling him that he looked perfectly okay and simply had to stop lying around doing nothing but feeling sorry for himself.

"I just couldn't get myself in gear. They couldn't understand that. I had no confidence.

They kept pushing me to do things and I kept hearing the Captain's put-downs over and over like a broken record. Nothing made sense. Everyone was bugging me to get going – 'Do something, anything – Just do it!' Pretty soon I felt like everyone knew what was in my head. I couldn't sleep. I couldn't get myself to ever try anything. I stayed in bed all day and then I started thinking about suicide. Finally, I took a whole bunch of pills – I passed out, landed in the hospital ER and they shipped me here to the VA hospital."

"So what are you *still* afraid of, David?" I asked after listening to his story. "What scares you now? In a way, that business about losing your brains was kind of a distraction, wasn't it? That was all to help you stop thinking those terrible thoughts that got you to the point of wanting to commit suicide, wasn't it?"

"I guess sometimes I still am afraid I'll get to feel so miserable again that I will want to kill myself. When I let myself think about all that happened, I don't feel like I deserve to live. That's what scares me. The Captain called us garbage, right? Well, we don't keep garbage around for long, do we? We get rid of garbage. We destroy it!"

"Whoa," I said. "Hold on a minute, David. What makes you think you're garbage? Just because some dumb CO said so? He's the one who deserved to be court- martialed. Not you."

Over the next few days, David could not, or would, not accept my arguments against his self-deprecating views about himself. Finally, two weeks before I was to have finished my tour of duty at the hospital, I tried an approach with David which had earlier been suggested by my supervisor.

"David, this whole business of your constantly criticizing yourself makes me think that you've got some special need to punish yourself. You won't accept my arguments about how unjustified it is for you to keep putting yourself down, so I've got to think you still *need* to put yourself down – like you're out to punish yourself for something. Why do you need to punish yourself? What did you do that was so terrible?"

"I should've thought by now you would have known the answer to that," David shrugged. "Can't you at least guess?"

"Got to be something to do with your POW experience?"

"Of course! I let myself be brainwashed, didn't I? They didn't try it with everyone, did they? Why did they pick me? They must have seen me as weak – no guts to stand up to them – garbage, like the Captain said." David's head dropped to his chest.

"Okay," I said. I had anticipated what he would say. "Let us allow for arguments sake that you are guilty. Guilty of having been weak, vulnerable – whatever, you were seen as an easy mark. okay?"

"Okay." David had lifted his head and was staring at me.

"So, let's say you're guilty as charged. Any God-damn court in the land upon having found you guilty would then impose a sentence, right?"

"What are you getting at?" David eyed me suspiciously.

"How long are you here? I mean on this ward – and the rest of the time since you were hospitalized?"

"A little over two years – but what's that got to do with my being guilty?"

"Just this – being here is like being in jail, right? You're confined to the ward. They lock the doors behind you. You're watched like you're in prison, right?"

"Yeah, so, I still don't see what you're getting at, "he said.

"You've already been incarcerated, David. Do you know what that means? It's like you've already been in jail for over two years! You were found guilty, David, and you've served time for it. You've been punished – as if the year you spent in a POW camp wasn't enough, you've done time, David – and more than enough to meet any court sentence which would have been imposed. Do you know what that means?"

I had David's attention. "No, not exactly – what does it mean?"

"Your sentence is over, David. You've been punished for your crimes against the nation, for personally being weak, for having been a turn-coat, for having given in. For whatever reason you can think of, you've done your time – it's over, it's all over! There's no need for you to be punished further, you don't need to punish yourself any longer. It's enough."

David let out a soft, low sigh. "I have to think more about that," he said, finally after a moment or two of saying nothing – he just stared down at his hands, resting on his knees. I left him there in the day room. Told him I'd check in with him the next morning. The strategy I had used, which my supervisor had recommended, was similar to a technique reported by a prominent psychotherapist who called it the "trick against the trick." I hoped it might have some impact with David.

Next morning, a somber David told me he had thought over what I had said, that at least in part, it made sense, and that he would request a meeting with Dr. Winters and the ward staff to see if they would agree to a weekend pass, so he could discuss it all further with his parents. I walked off the ward elated, my feet seemed like they were barely touching the corridor floor.

Soon afterward, I completed my assignment and left Katonah before David got his weekend pass. Dr. Winters had delayed granting the pass until he'd had a chance to observe David further and talk with him himself. But one of the ward attendants told me, the day I left, that David seemed intent on pursuing some sort of gradual discharge plan if his parents would agree to it.

Two months later I received a letter from David. He was still in the hospital. Dr. Winters had persisted in delaying matters further, but David thanked me "for putting things in perspective." He said that he was still going to pursue discharge, and then I had to laugh at his closing lines:

"By the way, that crap you told me about my having been punished enough for my sins, you must have got that from some book, right?" Then he added, "It doesn't matter though. Your idea that I had served enough time was what kind of worked anyway. So whatever happens here, I know I'm going to be okay. I want to thank you for that."

It was simply signed,

"David – an ex-POW."

I never heard from him again.

NO SNEERING ALLOWED

Lieutenant Colonel Peter R. Chernok leaned forward, his face red, his eyes bulging, his finger poking holes in the air, a few inches from my face. "You will not contradict my orders young trooper – Your Miss Browder goes back to the ward for shock treatments, and that's that! Do you heah?! Is that cleah?!"

"At least order a neurological, sir," I persisted. "She just doesn't look that depressed to me."

He turned back to me angrily. His face redder than before. Then he bared his teeth – he looked like a Texas Rattler poised to strike.

"Y'all lookin' to be coht-martialled?" he hissed. "Y'all aware, Private Logen, I kin send you up for in-so-bawd-en-nation. Y'all aware of that? Now," he thrust his finger at me again, "Are you questioning mah judgment? I seen Miss Browder on rounds, Private – and I'm telling you," he leaned forward and pounded his fist on his desk. "She's depressed!!"

I stepped back a bit. "I don't mean to question your judgment, Sir – but I thought this was a hospital, Sir – (my sarcasm wasn't well-concealed). Can't we still get a neurological on her – it might…"

Chernok interrupted. "Sergeant!" he yelled over to his secretary, seated a few feet away. "Get this young know-it-all out of here before I call the MPs!" He waved dismissively at me. "And you tell your Captain Greene I want to talk to him. Now get out of here!"

I shook my head. I must have glared at him before I turned to leave.

"Wait a minute. What's that look on your face?" he roared. "Are you sneering at me?! Don't you never sneer at me! Nevah! You evah do that again, and I will have you thrown in the Stockade! And one mo thing – you will come to attention and salute when I tell you to leave. Is that cleah, soldja?!"

"Yes Sir!" I saluted stiffly, wheeled about and began walking out. As I passed Sergeant Turner's desk, he glanced up, shrugged, and stared back at the papers on his desk. I knew him from the barracks. I knew how he felt about Chernok. Everyone in our clinic detested him. Everyone. Officers and enlisted men alike. They also had little respect for him as a psychiatrist.

Chernok had less than a year to go before he was due to retire. But he was still very much in command, reporting only to the Fort Sam base commandant and the Chief Medical Officer of Brooke Army Hospital. All of us, our Psychology Department, the rest of the Psychiatric Unit of the hospital, our outpatient clinic, neurology, all the other medical units on our Annex and all base personnel attached to those units – we all had to put up with Chernok. He was old, old Regular Army, eccentric, irascible, unpredictable, and, from what I'd heard, generally perceived as incompetent. But, again, this was the Army, and he was in charge.

Just before I was inducted into the Army, in the spring of 1953, I had completed my Master's degree in Psychology and briefly interned in one of the most highly regarded mental institutions, Hillside Hospital, in New York City. Then, while I was at Camp Kilmer in New Jersey, before I took basic training at Fort Dix, I was pulled out of indoctrination to work at the psychiatric clinic because of my skills as a psychological examiner. Then, after basic, in recognition of my graduate training as a psychologist, I was specially assigned to Brooke Army Hospital at Fort Sam Houston in San Antonio, Texas. I had, therefore, already had a taste of clinical work as a psychologist, so my assignment to Brooke, even though it meant going "overseas" to Texas, was something I looked forward to.

The flight down to San Antonio, aboard an old Army Troop Transport, was a bit bumpy, but otherwise uneventful. As we landed, though it was almost nightfall, I looked out expecting to see miles and miles of prairies, sagebrush, cactus and rolling tumbleweed. We debarked, after a short delay upon landing. So it was dark by then, and we were coming off the side of the plane facing away from the terminal. I couldn't see much, but the stars, as advertised, were certainly bright. I expected to see a stagecoach come round the plane to take us to the terminal building, where I'd heard we'd be met by a chorale group, the Daughters of the Alamo, who'd be there to sing "The Eyes of Texas are Upon You."

There was no stagecoach. And no one sang any sort of greeting to us. We were hustled off into an old Army Troop Carrier and wound up at the entry gate to Fort Sam Houston about a half hour later. We were soon settled into our two-story barracks homes, where our First Sergeant-in-Charge welcomed us, Army style, and, informed us that he was there to make us all feel comfortable. Fortunately, a few months later, my wife came down to join me and we moved off post. Meanwhile, I was feeling increasingly good about my work assignment to Brooke's Psychiatric Outpatient Clinic. Not unlike my experience as an intern at Hillside Hospital, I had begun to feel like I was once again part of an interdisciplinary team making joint decisions about patients' treatment programs. Consequently, it really upset me when I found myself involved in a dispute over a patient's diagnosis and treatment plan with Colonel

Chernok. That never would have happened at Hillside. We would have resolved our differences at a staff meeting.

I walked back down the hall from the Outpatient Clinic, upset and angry over Chernok's refusal to consider my request for a neurological exam as well as my diagnostic impressions in the Browder Case.

"That son of a bitch!" I slammed the Browder file on my desk and walked quickly over to Captain Greene's office, adjacent to our work area. He saw me coming and waved me in. Captain Charles Greene was also RA, but a psychologist first. He treated all of us non-coms like colleagues.

"From the look on your face," he said, "I guess I'm gonna get a call from Chernok. Didn't he listen at all?"

"Yeah, ten seconds' worth," I replied. "Then he puffed up and pulled rank on me. He even said if I persisted in recommending a neurological for Browder", a Pediatric nurse from one of the General hospital wards, " he'd have me up on charges for insubordination. I spent hours with her. I listened to everything she was complaining about. I studied her test results and went over them several times. I'm not wrong."

Greene sat back in his chair and sighed. "We've had to learn to coexist with Chernok. Lucky for us he's on his way out to pasture, but he's always at his worst if anyone challenges him – especially some young non-com like you, who questions his judgment. But don't worry," he said, "I can usually talk him down about anyone who bugs him – which, by the way, includes just about everyone here in the clinic."

"How have you survived?" I asked.

Greene laughed. "You know, that troubles me. I think maybe it's simply that he needs me to help keep the clinic from falling apart. He goes on quiet little rampages sometimes, even walks the halls with his riding crop, he's real RA – goes in and out of private consultation rooms without knocking, even interrupts therapy sessions unannounced. Once he walked in on one of my meetings with a patient and his family – he actually walked around the room checking for dust on the furniture – a God damned white glove inspection in the middle of my conference.

"How the hell does he get away with it? Can't you go over his head?"

"I've tried, actually – I've gone to the hospital Commander about him, about his inappropriate behavior. I was simply told to keep it quiet – that Chernok would be retiring soon and it wasn't worth making a fuss about."

"So, what can we do about the Browder case? He's pushing Shock for her, and if I'm right, that's the last thing she needs."

"Calm down, young trooper," said Greene, holding his hand up to cut me short.

"Hey, I've already been young-troopered enough today," I told him. "How can Chernok override us? It's unprofessional!"

Greene nodded. "That may be, but remember he outranks us all – and this is the United States Army. The chain of command is next to Godliness – it's a fact of life – haven't you learned that?

Greene sat back and looked out his office window for a moment, "You know the system can be worked in strange and wondrous ways," he said. He was smiling.

"What do you mean?" I asked.

Chernok rode you out about your recommendation for a neurological for Browder, right? He got pissed off at you for arguing against the immediate course of ECT he wanted, right? And he insists she's depressed, right?"

"So..." I was getting impatient.

"So, his order goes down to Neurology, to Lieutenant Cromwell, to set her up for Shock, but remember, Cromwell is from our department. So, I inform him that our most recent findings suggest that, preparatory to Shock, Browder ought to get a thorough neurological, EEG and all. That way, we've gone around Chernok, but we haven't actually countermanded his orders. In most hospitals they'd do a neurological as part of pre-Shock anyway, so Chernok doesn't even have to know about it. And, if anything turns up on the neurological exam to contraindicate shock treatment, we've got the data to block his order – okay?"

"You better believe it – it's okay," I nodded. "Is that how you became a Captain?"

Greene sat back and laughed. "Now, you better believe it. That's the Army way. You can always find a way to play the system when you have to."

As it turned out, Greene was right. Neurology found a benign tumor, a lump the size of a walnut, pressing on Miss Browder's pituitary gland. Shock treatments were, therefore, disallowed for fear of possibly exacerbating the growth of the tumor. Finally, she was operated on, the tumor was successfully removed and she was released a few months later, almost fully recovered.

A year later, a few months before I was discharged from the Army, Chernok finally was retired. He got a big pension and was granted permanent quarters on Post, along what we used to call "Old General's Row." I assumed that he'd soon be forgotten, but a month later I heard that he'd gotten into trouble. He had to be restrained by the Post's military police after attacking a grounds-maintenance man.

The story I heard was that he accused the workman of turning on the lawn sprinklers every morning, on purpose, when the Colonel went out to get his newspaper. The workman, a civilian groundskeeper, simply ignored him, and told Chernok he was crazy, so Chernok waited for him, and the next time he came to work the sprinklers, Chernok went after him with his riding crop. No charges against the Colonel were actually filed, but the report had it that Chernok made a real fool of himself.

To this day, I still have a vision of Chernok chasing the grounds-keeper down General's Row, yelling at him and menacing wildly with his riding crop. That image consoles me whenever I have a run-in with some irrational authority – and, especially, if I'm accused of sneering.

A MOMENT I'D LIKE
TO FORGET

At age 30, shortly after completing my graduate work in psychology and my military service in San Antonio, I began searching for my first full-time job, either at a VA hospital or some child guidance clinic or possibly as a school psychologist. I therefore was on my way to be interviewed in New London, CT for a child guidance position when I stopped in New Haven to visit a former supervisor and friend who was in charge of psychological services at a clinic there. When he learned about my job seeking, he laughed. "Wow. You are in luck! There is something happening at Yale, which I'm sure will interest you. They are looking for someone for a new position as consultant to a local school system, someone who can build a program of psychological services there, and also teach a course or two in Yale's graduate MAT program."

I couldn't believe what I was hearing. "I'd love it," I managed to say, "and teaching at Yale? What an opportunity. I'm not sure I'm up to it, but it sounds great!"

A few months later, after a series of lengthy interviews, I got the job. The Yale professors who met with me said they liked the fact that I had done some part-time work as a school psychologist and had taught graduate level courses at the University of Buffalo.

My parents went "gaga" over the Yale teaching part and called everyone they knew to tell them I was a Yale professor. My wife and I were also thrilled, but I had, meanwhile, learned that Yale's Graduate MAT students included some of the best young teachers recruited from all over the United States. That made me feel somewhat anxious to say the least. So when I was assigned to teach my first class in "Theories of Personality," I over-prepared. I spent many hours reviewing and revising my lecture notes and reread several sections of the texts I had used previously at Buffalo. Therefore, by the time I walked into my first Yale class I was confident, but still had some feelings of trepidation. I first met briefly with the MAT coordinator, an older woman who also taught some of the MAT courses, and then I introduced myself to the students, when all had been seated. I told them a little about my background and then I began to lecture.

"Much of the early work done," I began, "on the development of personality theory was introduced by three highly regarded psychologists. The first, John Dewey, I'm sure you've heard a lot about. The second, Christopher Angyal, was known as one of the originators of the Gestalt School of Psychology. The third was a famous neuropsychologist I had the honor of taking courses with at the City College of New York. His name was …" I paused, and a tiny voice in my head said, "You're not going to remember his name." Indeed, I suddenly drew a complete blank. I felt a wave of panic and embarrassment as I stared down at my notes on the podium, but I couldn't locate his name. Finally, I looked up at the class, all eyes expectantly waiting, and I stammered, "You know – I've forgotten his name!" Most of the students just stared at me. A few of them laughed. And then, his name, Kurt Goldstein, popped back into my head. I raised my arms, as if in surrender, shook my head and picked up where I'd left off.

The rest of my lecture went smoothly, but my embarrassment over forgetting Goldstein's name lingered. Later, the MAT coordinator came up to me as I was shuffling my notes away into my briefcase. "That was quite a moment there," she said. "You know, when you were just starting out – when you forgot Goldstein's name." Then she laughed. "Happens to me all the time. But nothing to get upset about. It's called being a 'forgetful' professor. Otherwise you did fine." I thanked her, and actually felt some relief. But as I left the classroom, I stopped for a second and mumbled to myself "but where the hell did that little voice come from?" I still don't know!

I HATE SHRINKS

Ironically, one of the very first clients referred to me when I first opened my private practice in Westport, was a teenager named Wendy who immediately informed me that she "hated shrinks" and had come to see me only because her parents had insisted upon it.

"Furthermore," she added, "just because they're paying for it, doesn't mean I have to talk!"

When I had arranged the appointment with her mother, I had no idea that Wendy was so opposed to seeing me, or to any other therapist for that matter. Over the phone, her mother had said that Wendy didn't like being referred for therapy by her school principal, but I hadn't expected Wendy's outburst, nor did I anticipate her refusing to either shake my hand or sit in the chair I motioned her to. Instead she sat down on the floor in the far corner of the room and hid her face under the floppy-felt hat she was wearing.

"I'm not talking," she repeated. "You can say what you want – you can ask me anything you want – I don't have to answer!" Her voice trailed off to muttering about having to stay the full hour only because she didn't have a ride home.

I hesitated. I didn't know what to say. I was a bit upset, and a little annoyed that she was so dismissive toward me before I'd even said anything. But, I sensed that if I tried to say something about how angry she seemed, or if commented about what she'd said, it would likely irritate her more. So, I didn't say anything.

After a long moment or two, she said, "So Shrink, aren't you going to ask me a bunch of questions? Isn't that your job?"

I laughed. "You know, you haven't given me many options. You've made it clear you don't want to be here, and you've said you don't want to talk. I could ask you lots of questions, but if you refuse to answer, what's the point? Shrinks are trained to be good listeners, so I'm listening. You got anything to say?"

Under the hat, I heard Wendy say, "Hmmm." Then she lifted her head and stared at me. "I didn't expect that," she said.

"What *did* you expect?" I asked.

Wendy told me she thought I would be plying her with all kinds of questions, "nosing about to find out why I'd been told to see a therapist, and trying to analyze me – and all that stuff."

I told her that I would prefer to get to know her first – before "plying."

She got quiet again. And little more was said for the rest of our session. She remained hunched down in her corner. But when she left, she shook my hand and nodded when I said I hoped to meet with her again.

Wendy had just turned sixteen, a junior at a local private high school for girls. When I met with them, the staff there described her as an extremely bright but underachieving student. They said her work showed "great promise", when she seemed interested in the assigned topic, or liked the teacher, but that was rare. Most of the time, they said, she seemed moody and at times was even disrespectful, ignoring teachers' efforts to motivate her. She was also described as "pretty much a loner," rarely seen in the company of any of the other girls, most often sitting alone in the cafeteria, and that sometimes she expressed disdain regarding other student's comments in class. The Principal said she was concerned that Wendy's grades were so poor, that despite their efforts to get her to do the work they expected she could handle easily, they might have to ask her parents to transfer her elsewhere. The staff expressed hope that therapy would help ease her moodiness, which they thought was symptomatic of depression, and that Wendy might become more of the student they expected she could be.

When I interviewed Wendy's parents, which she said was "okay as long as she didn't have to sit in the same room with them," they presented an even bleaker picture. They said she quarreled a lot with her older brother and sister and that she'd often spend long hours alone in her room. They were somewhat surprised to hear that the school staff thought she was depressed, but they did acknowledge that Wendy often seemed to be in some sort of "blue funk."

"She's also recently lost interest in some of the things she used to enjoy," her mother said – "like horses. She's always been crazy about horses, you know, ever since she was old enough to ride them. She would even spend her weekends down at the stables, helping out any way she could – feeding them, washing them down, even exercising them when the people there would let her. Sometimes, instead of doing her homework, she would draw or doodle horses. And, at dinnertime, all she could talk about was horses, horses, horses, until we'd tell her to shut up."

Wendy's mother said Wendy had owned her own horse since she was twelve years old. It was kept at the stable and Wendy used to help pay for it all by working there on weekends. "But now," she said, "even Max, her horse –- short for Maximillian, doesn't seem to interest her much when she's feeling blue."

I asked if Wendy had any trouble sleeping. And, I was told that Wendy *did* have a problem sleeping through the night, that she would wake her mother complaining that she couldn't sleep, and that, by morning, she often seemed exhausted.

There were other problems. Both parents complained that Wendy had become hard to reach, but that they assumed she was going through adolescent adjustment problems and that they thought therapy might help pull her out of her blue funks. They also said that if I determined that Wendy was really depressed, that they would be willing to consider any psychiatric intervention I might recommend regarding the need for prescribed medications.

Wendy expressed absolutely no interest in anything I'd heard about her from either the school staff or her parents. She pooh- poohed my efforts to tell her, came into the next couple of sessions each time informing me that she was there "under protest," had nothing to say, went to her corner, slouched down into it, pulled her floppy hat down over her face, and remained quiet for most of the hour.

I knew, from prior experiences I'd had with depressed adolescents, that if I confronted her about her resisting my efforts to get her to talk with me, I'd get nowhere. I decided to try something different.

"You know, I like your hat," I said. "Is it new?"

Wendy shrugged.

"The color matches my rug."

"Fuck you," she said.

"I'm married," I said.

"What? What's that got to do with anything?"

"Well, just so you know, I'm married – and besides, it's not ethical for therapists to have sex with their clients."

"Who said anything about sex?" she said. "I said fuck you… that's like bug off, get off my back – it's got nothing to do with sex!"

"Oh, I'm sorry."

"Sorry? Sorry for what?"

"Sorry I misunderstood you."

Wendy looked up and saw that I was smiling. That perplexed her, but then she smiled too, for the first time.

"What is it with you, Shrink? You're apologizing, but smiling at the same time. I think you need a shrink."

Then she laughed. The silliness of our interchange had broken the ice. At least for the moment, a moment I tried to prolong.

"You know, you have an infectious laugh – it's hard to resist."

"Really?" she softened a bit more. "No one's ever said that to me."

"I guess I'm not surprised."

"What do you mean?"

"Simply that I don't think you let too many people hear you laugh – or see you cry."

"Why should I?" she answered. "There aren't too many people out there who understand what's funny and what's not."

"You wanna try me?"

"Why should I?"

"Because you might find out I'm not like the people out there, who don't think like you."

"Oh, and you think you do?"

"Try me."

"What could you know about what makes me laugh or what makes me want to cry?"

"Because I've been there – feeling down and not feeling understood, I mean – feeling apart from what others usually think or say. Try me – you've got nothing to lose."

"I'll think about it." She said nothing more for the rest of our session.

I had the feeling that the door had closed, that maybe I had said something to close it, but that there was no point in pushing further that day. I hoped we might start the next session on a different footing, but when Wendy came in for her next appointment it seemed like nothing had changed. She sat in her corner again and hid behind her hat for at least the first 20 minutes. I felt I had to chance probing a bit, even if it risked closing her off entirely.

"You know, for a while last session, I thought you were getting close to trusting me."

"Whatever gave you that idea?"

"I don't know," I answered. "Maybe it was because we found the same silly things to laugh at."

"Yeah, but then you started with that 'try me' crap."

"I was afraid of that – I figured I screwed up somewhere."

"Not really – something you said made me think. Like you weren't just out to get me to talk so you could tell my parents you were finally getting through to me, you know. I thought about it later while my mother drove me home. What did you mean when you said you've been there? What's that all about?"

"Well, I don't know enough really about you, Wendy – at least not from you, or anything you've said so far. But if you're having a hard time about the things I think may be troubling you, that is – if I'm right – then I *have* been there, I have been through the blues over stuff, like what maybe bothering you. I got through it, finally – and my hunch is that you can too!"

"Hey, nice speech – what makes you so sure about me?"

"Because you're a smart kid, Wendy, smarter than most, and you evidently are a sensitive, caring person too. I heard about how you love horses for example."

"Horses aren't people," she exclaimed. "They don't give you shit like people do. You can't trust people. You take good care of a horse and he's your friend forever. People use you for what they can get, and then they're outta here!"

"Hasn't there been anyone for you, anyone you could trust, someone who stayed loyal when you needed them?"

"Never!" She pulled her floppy hat off, crushed it in her hands and pulled it down over her head again, sighing heavily as she resumed staring down at the rug's fringes. She had stopped talking again, but she'd given me some ideas to work with. During our next session, we got further into what got her angry – what got her depressed, and what led up to her mistrusting people.

"How can you trust anyone when all they're interested in is themselves?" she said, as our next session began. I noticed that she had chosen to sit in the chair opposite her usual slouching corner. Her floppy hat still covered most of her face, though. I told her that I thought most people her age tended to be self-involved, that it was part of growing up, and that there was a good chance that she'd be meeting more people, as she grew older, who might be more genuinely interested in her, maybe even as much as she was in them. I argued that she needn't give up on everyone in general – not quite yet. Then I shut up.

Wendy began talking more and more during the next few sessions about her experience with the other kids at school. "Sometimes I think I've got bad breath, or some social disease," she said. "I ask somebody something and see that she's looking away or she rushes away like she has an important message for someone at another table. Then, one girl, who I thought liked me, told me she thought I was weird. When I asked why, she just shrugged and said everybody thought I was weird. Then, when I asked her what she meant, she told me it was hard to explain but that the other girls thought I was not just a little strange, but that I just had a rep as being unapproachable – you know, really, really weird!"

Wendy looked up at me from under her hat. "Do you think I'm weird?"

I had to think quickly. "Yeah, maybe, but – so what if you're weird?" I answered.

"Shrinks aren't supposed to say that to their patients." She was smiling.

"Maybe not, but frankly I find your kind of weird intriguing. Except for how you wear your hat, I tend to find people who others call weird – more interesting."

"I thought you said you liked my hat?" she said.

"Actually I do – but it's the way you hide behind it that probably makes you look unapproachable. Did your friend at school say anything about that?"

"No, she didn't spell out any other details – just said I was very weird and that everyone said so."

"Do you want to do something about being more approachable?" I asked.

"Oh no – well, maybe. I'm not exactly overloaded with friends these days. But on the other hand, maybe I do overdo it. And yet, I don't want to be a conformist either, watching those lemmings at school follow whoever sounds off the loudest – it makes me want to puke."

"Neither too aggressive, nor a follower be. And above all else to thine own self be true…" I mused.

"That's Shakespeare isn't it? From Hamlet I think; we just read it in school."

"Correct Madam! I misquoted it a bit, but you get the idea. You know, you can maintain your integrity without having to go from one extreme to another."

"Okay, Shrink, what do I do next?" she sighed.

Our next few sessions were the most important of all. I listened carefully to what Wendy said she would try to do to stop being so avoidant of others at school, and to be more responsive in class. It was slow going but gradually, her efforts proved successful, and she began reporting back to me that she was getting more and more involved in a small circle of friends who, she told me, she enjoyed being with. I became less of an advisor, and more someone who shared and laughed with her over her "coming out" experiences. Then, after a while, Wendy's parents reported that she was a "changed kid" at home, more talkative, and less frequently caught up in her "blue funks."

A month later, I suggested that we meet less frequently. We agreed that she had obviously resolved enough matters on her own, and that we might only get together as needed.

Wendy didn't hesitate. "Yeah, we could do that," she said. " I can call you, I guess, when anything comes up that I need to consult with you about – like at school, or if anything at home gets to me too much."

"That's the idea," I said. "We could go on meeting like we have, until you're an old lady (at which she smiled broadly), but let's meet when you really need to go over something that comes up that's giving you a hard time. From what you've told me, and from all we've hashed over, I think you're ready to take on the cruel, cold world pretty much on your own, but when or if you need me, I'm not going anywhere. I'll be here."

Wendy gave me a big hug, smiled, and waved back at me as she walked out of my office. I felt a surge of warm accomplishment, but at the same time, a bit of regret, which I recognized as the kind of personal reaction psychologists are supposed to have had trained out of them.

Over the years, since we first worked together, Wendy called or came in from time to time for a "therapy fix." She struggled through some difficult times, first over breaking ties with her family when she went off to college, then concerning a few difficult, frustrating relationships with guys she met along the way. But in her last telephone call, Wendy informed me that she was living with a man a few years older than herself, who she respected, who she said was extremely intelligent and supportive. She said he was someone who encouraged her career aspirations, unlike her former boyfriends. "This time, things look good," she assured me. "By the way," she added, "I'm thinking of doing graduate work in Sociology, maybe even become a Social Worker. But don't get a big head about it," she added. "I still can't stand Shrinks."

I'M LISTENING

Scottie Wyman, one of the brightest kids I'd ever tested, was about to be expelled from St. Peter's Academy for calling his gym teacher "a fucking Neanderthal."

When Mrs. Wyman called, she asked if I could intervene.

"We don't know what to do with him anymore. Sorry to bother you again but this is the third time this semester he's cursed at a teacher. They've had it with him. They even told us to start looking for another private school for him. What should we do?"

"Is it definite that he's out of St. Peter's?" I asked.

"Looks like it. They say he's been insubordinate once too often. They recognize he's a gifted kid. They read your report, but they, the Dean I mean, said that they just can't tolerate his behavior anymore. He said that Scottie only worked for the teachers he liked, and thumbed his nose at everyone else. He said that they just couldn't tolerate his unwillingness to abide by their rules."

"What do you and Harry think, Judy? Do you see Scottie as that much of a problem?"

"Well, a little maybe," said Judy. "Scottie's our kid. I tend to think they're too rigid and uptight at St. Peter's, so I can see Scottie's side of it. But then I'm his mother."

"So what are you worried about? We can find a school that caters to gifted kids, one that also has a good drama program, and see if it makes a difference. He still interested in becoming an actor?"

"Oh, yeah," Judy answered. "He loves it. But it still makes Barry a little crazy. The two of them can't even talk about it. They really don't talk about much. You know that problem, but I'm for whatever he'd like to do with his life. I just worry ..."

"About what, Judy?"

"You know — I worry about him, that's all — you know — that he'll never be accepted anywhere."

"You still think he's got some kind of bad seed, don't you?"

"Well, I know you don't think so, but I can't help worrying about him that way. My brother was diagnosed as Schizophrenic, and he's still in Creedmore. My father had it, and you know <u>my</u> history. How can he miss?"

"Listen, Judy," I said, "Let me talk with Scottie, if you think you can get him to come in. What do you think? If he's willing to come in, I can see him Friday."

"I think you're the only person he might be willing to talk to. He enjoyed taking all those tests with you last year. He thinks you're cool. I'll ask him and get back to you."

Scottie came in on Friday at the time we arranged. He seemed sullen, and, at first, said very little. I decided to be direct with him. Most fourteen year olds I'd worked with, like Scottie, seemed to appreciate my being up front with them.

"St. Peter's is about to give you the heave, Scottie. Your mother told me about all the problems they say you've created, which they claim they can't tolerate anymore. But, I want to hear your side of it. If you really don't want to talk about it, I can understand that, but I'm here to listen. I assume no one forced you to come back to see me, so what's the story?"

Scottie was quiet for a few more minutes. I could have prodded with more comments or observations, but I chose to stay silent and wait him out. Finally, after staring down at his feet awhile, he glanced up at me.

"This is off the record, right? I mean it's confidential — no one gets to know what I tell you, not even my parents, right?"

"Right! Unless you're planning to do yourself in, or some other dirty deed. Then I have to break confidence to save your soul. That's my rule. Everything else you want to keep between us, stays here. Agreed?"

"Yeah — agreed," he muttered barely loud enough for me to hear him.

"What do you want to know?"

"Your turn," I said. "What do you want to tell me?"

"They're assholes!" Scottie exclaimed. "Every last one of them. Taggart. He's the gym teacher. He's the biggest asshole . . . and Dean Parker. He keeps saying he's trying to help me, but he doesn't know shit. He only listens to what those jack-ass teachers of his, like Taggart say."

"Keep going. I'm listening."

"What's the use? They are all jerks! All they understand is their own stupid rules. I'm glad I'm outa there."

"What rules, Scottie?"

They've got rules for everything. Dumb, stupid, jerky rules — for everything!" he repeated.

"Rules you broke? Like what Scottie?" I asked again.

Like never talking back to a teacher. Like never asking questions unless you raise your hand to be recognized — stupid, dumb rules."

"Is that what happened? You talked out in class when you weren't supposed to? And you're getting bounced for that?"

"Well — more than that, I guess — I blew it with Taggart — called him a Neanderthal, and he sent me to the Dean.

"What happened?"

"Taggart is our gym teacher, but he also teaches Hygiene. They call it Health Values. Anyway, he was telling everyone to read the Bible for the truth about evolution and I asked if he'd ever heard of the Scopes trial. He started carrying on about how belief is more important than science, that the Scopes trial never proved anything, and then — he comes at me — didn't I believe in God! Really, he comes over and gets in my face and asks if I believe in God, Can you believe that shit?"

"St. Peter's is a private, parochial school. I wouldn't ever approve of his doing that, but yeah, I can believe it."

"Well, I lost it! I told him that Adam and Eve was bullshit, and that if he believed that crap he was a Neanderthal."

"A fucking Neanderthal, right?"

Scottie looked at me, and smiled, I just smiled back. Then he relaxed and we talked about what happens when you challenge authority, especially in schools like St. Peter's, where teachers are likely to try to promote the party line. We ended up talking about the probability that transferring to a different private school might make sense for him, especially if he didn't want to go back to the public school he'd attended up until fourth grade. I told him I'd do some research about schools he and his parents might like to check out, "At fourteen," I said, "You're still probably better off looking at other schools in our area rather than going off to a boarding school,"

I told him I thought he might have a hard time in some boarding schools.

"What do you mean?" he asked, "I'm not really interested in going away, but what makes you think I'd have a hard time?"

"Because when I listen to you, Scottie, I hear someone very young, someone much smarter than most people walking around out there, someone with huge potential for doing big things, but someone who already sees himself as very different, and not necessarily likeable – different."

"What do you mean?"

"Until you're older, Scottie, and more confident about what you believe, or what you choose to do, you're going to run into a whole lot of Taggarts, and others like Taggart who are in positions of authority and who can make your life miserable."

"So what — I can handle myself."

"If you're away at some boarding school, away from your family, your friends, away from people you can fall-in on and back you up, you may not find someone willing to hear you out, let alone do battle for you. You think you feel different now, Wow — you ain't seen nuttin'! You're not even a contender yet." I let my voice trail off, like a defeated boxer announcing his eventual comeback. Scottie laughed. I thought he'd appreciate the metaphor.

"But I'm doing the talking again. What about it, Scottie, can you tell me that you don't already feel different from almost everyone else? Especially in a school like St. Peter's. Don't you often feel marginal, you know, like on the outside looking in?"

"I think that's called projecting, Doc."

"Ok," I laughed. "Maybe it is. I've been there. I did that. But isn't that what's eating at you? What made you curse out Taggart like you did? In his own classroom, on his own turf ... that was a loser, Scottie, You know you had to lose that one."

Scottie admitted his frequent feelings of alienation. He did, indeed, already feel like a marginal man. He had only one friend, a girl he'd known from grade school, She was a year older than him and lived a few houses away on their cul-de-sac in Weston, a wealthy Connecticut suburban community in Fairfield County. They were just close friends, but were avid computer nuts.

"We surf together," he said. "Cheaper than skiing -- and no waiting in lines for the lifts."

But that was it. The kids at St. Peter's treated him like "a nerd," told him he was "just too weird" and that he was a "smart-ass." One upper classman even called him a "fag."

I took a chance. "Well <u>are</u> you so inclined? I mean gay-friendly. I doubt you've had much sex yet."

Scottie seemed startled. He looked at me archly, but then quickly relaxed again. "Nah, he was just being a jerk. I told my homeroom class one day that I was a member of the Gay Liberation Movement, but that was just to get a rise out of the teacher, that's all. I guess he heard about it."

"Why the hell did you do that?"

"Just a gag. Someone said something about a gay bashing they'd seen on· TV and our teacher sat there looking horrified that anyone would ever bring that up in class."

"See what I mean, Scottie? The gays of the world would love you for doing that. And if you ever do serious theater, you'll have lots of friends. But right now, that's just asking for trouble. If you were away in a boarding school where most people were intolerant of gays they'd make your life a living hell."

"Okay Doc, I get the point. Where do we go from here?"

"Well, if it's okay with you, let me get your parents in with you next time, so we can talk about what's out there for you to transfer to, okay?"

"Agreed," said Scottie.

As soon as the Wymans sat down, Judy nodded toward Scottie and with a wry smile told me ... "Scottie says you'd have no problem with him being gay — that is, if he was gay."

I laughed and glanced at Scottie. A big grin had spread across his face.

"Yeah, right," I answered. "But you need to know, Judy, the whole mental health profession has done a 180° turn on homosexuality since the late 80s. Hardly anyone looks at gays anymore as pathological. That's the majority opinion among professionals now, but that's not the whole world yet. Practically all of my gay clients, including a few who are now my friends, still get crazed by all the homophobia out there." I grinned back at Scottie — a fleeting exaggerated grin, "Why are you making trouble?" I told him.

Scottie laughed. Judy smiled broadly, but Harry looked glum. Judy had told me when she had called for the appointment that they had discussed what Scottie had told them about our meeting, including our discussion about gays. She said Harry was upset that his kid might be gay. She said he always had been troubled about that with Scottie because of Scottie's interest in acting, but couldn't talk about it. I decided to let that matter drop until a later time.

"We are gathered…" I said in as formal a way as I could muster. Scottie laughed in appreciation – "to contemplate another academic course of action for Sir Scott here who has chosen to alienate most of his present world by vigorously thumbing his nose at the likes of Mr. Taggart and good Dean Parker. Let us therefore consider the options available." I dropped the pronouncement mode. "I've found out about one school in particular, about twenty minutes up the line toward Danbury, but what have you explored?"

Judy said, "I think we may be talking about the same school. Do you mean the Whitman school in Redding?"

"Yes," I replied. "It's a small school, not too well known. It caters to bright kids who are underachievers, but not Special Ed., and it's especially good for kids who are interested in the Performing Arts. They've got a great drama program and some sports, like soccer which I know Scottie is good at, but they are also a school that tolerates kids who have been in trouble elsewhere, as long as they' re not too oppositional."

"What does that mean?" asked Harry. "The Dean at St. Peter's called Scottie oppositional."

"Yes, but that was St. Peter's. They're not exactly known for bending their rules for anyone. In fact, they're probably much too rigid on that score about anyone who steps out of line. Whitman is just the opposite. From what I hear, they actually encourage kids to question anything and everything. They don't let everyone yell out all at once, but they also don't require raising your hand to be called on. I think Scottie could handle that.

It's a whole different atmosphere and some of the kids are quite bright." I glanced at Scottie. "What say you, sir?"

"Sounds good to me. Can we visit it?" he asked.

"Yes, right away, in fact. The headmaster will want to get your records from St. Peter's and the testing I did with you last year, but he thought Whitman might work for you. And, he wasn't looking for customers. He said they're almost filled-up for the fall."

"There's one other school I thought might be good for Scottie," said Judy. "It's the Rushmore School in White Plains — and it's only a forty minute drive."

"It's worth a look," I said. "Beautiful grounds, and it has a reputation as a terrific prep school, but like its name implies, it tends to be very achievement-oriented and more conformist. Anyway, it won't hurt to take a look."

We then talked further about their expectations for Scottie. As I'd figured, the gay issue still lingered. But it was Judy who raised it, not Harry who I had anticipated would be more troubled by any hint that Scottie might ever become gay. She said, "You know, everyone thought my brother was gay. That it was one of the reasons he became Schizophrenic." She glanced furtively at Scottie who was watching her intently. "Scottie kids around about being gay, I know, mostly to provoke people. But is there any chance he's got some of those genes?"

Harry was also staring at her. His mouth was open, like she'd expressed his biggest fear — right in front of Scottie.

"Suppose for argument's sake, he did turn out gay, would that change how you feel about him?" I asked.

"Well certainly – uh, of course not – it's just that…" Harry's stammering clearly revealed the significance of the issue for him.

Scottie turned to his father. "Yeah, Dad — suppose I was really gay — so what then — would you disown me?"

Harry regained his composure. "No, of course not —" Then he hesitated. "It would worry me Scottie to think you were gay, Oh, not because of how most people view gays. That's not how I feel, Scottie." He leaned over and put his hand on Scottie's arm. "It's because —" Harry swallowed. His voice broke "It's because I don't want to see you get hurt anymore. That's all. People can be cruel, Scottie." Harry couldn't say anything more.

Judy was crying. Scottie stared at his father like he had never seen him before, He placed his hand over his father's hand, still resting on his arm.

"It's okay, Dad — it's okay. I never thought you felt that way." Then he stood up, bent over toward both his parents and gestured toward himself with both hands. "C'mon," he said softly. "Hey, this is me, I'm not gay — there's nothing to worry about!" Then Scottie looked back at me as he leaned over to comfort his mother who was still crying.

"I guess if I was gonna be gay, this is the family to be in, right?"

"Right," I nodded, I felt choked up myself.

Scottie went to the Whitman School the following fall. I got a call from Judy who told me that he had settled in very nicely and was doing fine. She thanked me for all the help she felt I'd provided, not only for getting them out of the St. Peter's mess, but for helping them come to grips with some of their fears about Scottie. "You know that last meeting we had with you left us pretty shook up. But it opened up a whole lot of things we hadn't been able to talk about before. We really want to thank you for that. It must make you feel good when that happens."

A HOLE IN HIS HEAD

Ray Morris had a hole in his head. A large surgically created hole, with a metal plate temporarily installed to keep his brain lobes s in place until some new bone tissue might grow in and take over the job. Ray had had a cerebra-vascular accident or CVA. He had, in fact, almost died on the operating table, but was now given a good chance to live if a procedure called a "shunt" worked effectively to reduce and control the build-up of brain fluids following his operation.

Shortly after his operation, I visited Ray at Yale New Haven Hospital. He looked barely alive, his head was bandaged and there was a mass of tubes going in and out of his body. He looked so poorly, I was sure he wouldn't survive, but he did. He also was doing remarkably well during his rehabilitation. Nevertheless, I was a bit surprised to get a call from him so soon.

"Do you think I'm gonna get it all back?" Ray asked. It was a few months after he'd been discharged from the hospital. He was still on out-patient rehabilitation and, reportedly, was quickly regaining most of the speech he'd temporarily lost. But he said he wanted to see me. He wanted to resume the counseling sessions we'd been having for some time before his CVA.

"The report I got from Dr. Novarro looks good, Ray," I told him when he came in. Most of the neuro-psych assessments suggest you've already regained 80% functioning; more so on the left, that's your language processing side, but you're coming back strong in general. Novarro says he wants to do some retesting with you in the fall, but he expects you will have recovered just about all of your language skills by then and, at least, 90% of your abstract reasoning ability. He said that you're well on your way to a complete recovery."

"It sounds good," said Ray. But he didn't sound enthusiastic. His voice was subdued, and he looked a little down.

"It's all good," I continued, "but Ray, something's bothering you – what's up?"

"I'm scared that it could happen again," he said.

I didn't say anything right away. Then I sighed... "I guess I'm not surprised Ray – go ahead, I'm listening."

Ray had been looking down at his knees. Then he looked up and smiled half-heartedly. "I guess I'm worried that the axe will fall again". He paused."But, at least it beats dying," His voice trailed off.

"Yes, you could say that," I said.

"I did say that," and Ray started to laugh.

"Ahhh – at least you're getting your sense of humor back."

"Oh, what the hell," Ray sat up. "I've got Peggy---- and she's pregnant, and we're gonna have our first kid soon, and my old paintings have started to sell again. So if I can get drawing again, maybe I can do more painting again. Maybe what I ought to do is just relax and go with the flow?"

"Why not start painting right away? Even if you don't have all your drawing skills back, at least you can do Jackson-Pollack stuff. How about that, Ray? You can get into a whole new art form – maybe you'll even sell more of your work that way – how about that?"

Ray eyed me archly; then he smiled again. "Therapists aren't supposed to give advice, and you're sure not supposed to make fun," he said. "You're supposed to be supportive. Hey, I'm still scared stiff!"

"There, there," I said, in mock consolation. "I shall continue to listen. But seriously, if I can get you to see the craziness in all your worrying and get your sense of humor working again, that could help. You're the guy who always says you can see the ridiculousness in situations you can't control. And Ray, this is one you really can't control!"

"There's nothing I can do about it, huh?"

"Nothing, nada Senor, Nichts!"

Novarro says getting past a CVA is likely to be worrisome well after people are perfectly okay again. It's like you got clobbered out of nowhere, without warning, so you expect it can happen the same way again."

"But you know what a control freak I am."

"But of course!" I said. "Listen Ray, it's a scary deal, but again, it's clearly beyond your control. So now you listen to me. If that's going to be very hard for you to accept, we can work on that. In fact, that can be what we really try to tackle for awhile. What about it, Ray?"

As the months passed, we returned time and again to the idea that, apart from exercising, watching his blood pressure and his general health, Ray could do little about the danger of another CVA. His problem was genetically determined, the distinct possibility of his having a further CVA was clear. His father, who had been a train conductor, keeled over and died of a stroke, which may have really been a CVA, while collecting tickets one morning on Metro-North. Ray's father was only 38 when he died and he left Ray and his two younger sisters in bad financial shape. His mother never got over it, so Ray had to often assume the role of both parents, and he became a surrogate father to his younger sisters all during their teen years. His efforts to control his and the family's circumstances, back then, he said, made him the control freak he said he was, but that wasn't about to change his inherited predisposition or his current fears. Therefore, helping Ray come to grips with that reality became our prime objective.

Prior to Ray's CVA, our focus had been on reducing his compulsivity, so that his control needs didn't appreciably interfere with his artistic creativity and/or his family life. We now needed to switch gears a bit and focus instead on how he might best overcome his recurring fear of being struck down again. After a couple of months Ray was still struggling.

"You know, I can be in the middle of doing something, like in our birthing class, and I get all shaky. It's always there, like my own sword of Damocles, waiting to take me out — like that!" Ray tried to snap his fingers, but couldn't, and that upset him. "When the hell will that come back?"

"You mean snapping your fingers?"

"Yeah."

"Is your drawing any better?"

"Yeah, it's coming."

55

"Well, that's what counts. Walking through the Yellow pages can wait."

"What?" Then Ray burst out laughing.

"I assume you got the point?"

"Yeah, how can I miss – okay," he sighed, "I'll take it one day at a time – but spare me the cute jokes."

"Why?" I answered, "if it gets back your perspective. Would you prefer my leaning close and saying, 'there-there?'" I leaned over and patted him on the knee.

Ray smiled. "Well — no, certainly not if you charge extra."

A few sessions later, Ray came in asking for anything he could work on, like a behavioral prescription for how he might deal with his apprehensiveness.

"Anything to help ward off the sword," he said. He then reminded me about a procedure I'd once suggested to him, a strategy developed by Jay Haley, the author of "Ordeal Therapy," which Ray had rejected when I'd first mentioned it. It involved what Haley called "focused worrying" and it was a technique which, as I'd outlined, actually put his compulsive need-to-control to work for him.

The plan called for Ray setting his alarm for a wake-up at 2 A.M. every morning. Then, upon awakening, he had to devote 20 minutes, and no less than 20 minutes, to *hard* worrying about anything he recalled which had troubled him during the previous day, particularly worrying about dying from another CVA, or about becoming seriously disabled. During those 20 minutes, he was to ignore all other thoughts except his worries about dying or becoming debilitated – he had to force himself to think of nothing else. Then, once he could do that, he was free to go back to sleep. In addition, the procedure required that he put all such troublesome thoughts aside whenever they occurred during the day. In other words, he was to defer all worrying about future CVAs, etc. until the prescribed 20 minutes of wake-up time at 2:00 AM. That was the time to be devoted to such worries – and no other time.

"That way," I said, "You won't be denying your worries, or evading them, you will be purposefully addressing them, but at an appointed time for appropriate consideration. It's like doing your worrying more efficiently."

"And that way, contractually, I agree to defer on worrying when it distracts me during the day or from stuff I have to do."

"Precisely!"

"I love it," said Ray. "It's the kind of idiotic idea that may help me keep things which I can't control in perspective."

"I think you've got it," I laughed. "By George, you've got it!"

Ray agreed to give it a try, and we set our next appointment for two weeks later. But a few days before we were to meet again, I got a call from him.

"Let's skip over another week, okay? I want to work on this awhile longer, but I have to tell you, it's working. It's really working!"

In his book, Haley said that this sort of ordeal, when it worked, worked because it penalized obsessive behavior (like Ray's pointless worrying) by making the consequences of such behavior especially burdensome. The procedure also helped underscore the irrationality of Ray's worrying (about things he couldn't control at all), by forcing him to hyperfocus on such worries at a particularly undesirable time.

An important outcome of Ray's having engaged in the prescribed ordeal he agreed to, was that we were eventually able to address other purposes served by Ray's apprehensiveness. He gradually came to realize that his obsessing over dying from another CVA was actually keeping him from more actively pursuing plans for other important events. For example, his CVA preoccupation had served to keep him from resolving any ambivalent feelings he had over having his first child, which Peggy was due to deliver in a few months. His preoccupations were also keeping Ray from making the final arrangements for the first exhibition of his paintings at a friend's gallery, arrangements he might otherwise have felt anxious about.

When Ray came in the next time, we really got down to work. I reminded him that even before his CVA, and long before Peggy became pregnant, his fears about ever having a child had plagued him. We discussed his always having been concerned that he might pass on his inherited predisposition to brain trauma, and we recalled that it had taken him and Peggy a while to resolve that concern so that they might relax and begin to try to have children. That old apprehensiveness had come roaring back since his actual CVA and, therefore, those issues needed to be resolved all over again. Ray's fears had also actually gotten in the way of practical planning, like buying baby furniture and fixing up the baby's room in their new house. He was now able to see all that more clearly, enough so that he and Peggy were now doing more of the practical preparing necessary for the baby, planning he had previously tended to put off "till he was feeling stronger and more up to it."

"We're actually, I mean *I'm* actually beginning to enjoy all that stuff. You know, like painting and papering the kid's room, shopping for furniture, all of that — I couldn't get going on it before."

"Well, if you get blocked again, you know what has to be done, don't you?"

"No, not the 2 A.M. worrying routine — not that — anything but that!"

Ray felt so good about the progress he'd made, we decided to discontinue our regular therapy sessions and meet only as needed. I got a call from him several months later, well after I received the birth announcement about their son.

"Hey, Doc, you gotta come see our kid. He's already pulling himself up in his crib. He's really wonderful." Ray went on and on about the joys of fatherhood.

"How are *you* doing?" I was finally able to ask.

"Well, if you really want to know, Peggy and I are exhausted. The baby is just beginning to sleep through the night, but really we are as happy as can be."

"No problems?" I asked. "No worrying? Hey I've got a special on phobias."

"No thanks," he yelled into the phone. "I've quit on that fear-of-dying stuff. No time for it. Now, I just worry about our kid. You know, stuff like whether or not he eats enough. He was colicky the first couple of months. We got through that okay, but now I worry that he doesn't eat enough. Our doctor says he's doing fine, but he looks kinda thin." Then, there was a pause.

"You know, I oughta come in and talk about that, Doc? Maybe I'm worrying about him too much."

OUR WORST FEAR

For therapists, perhaps the most difficult and worrisome clients to work with are those who have attempted suicide, those who threaten to take their own lives and those who may otherwise be considered suicide risks.

Early in my own practice, I enrolled in a family therapy center for continuing education and, while there, I often got together with other therapists in the program to compare notes about our experience. My most vivid recollection from those informal sessions was when one of us, who had only recently started his practice, described his horror and dismay when one of his adolescent clients tried to hang himself.

"Had his father not walked in and cut him down," John said, "he would have been gone. I had been working with him only a few weeks and I was devastated. It still shakes me up whenever I think it was my fault. No one actually blamed me, but I sure as hell couldn't stop blaming myself. It was on *my watch!*"

We were stunned by how upset John was, and we tried to reassure him that what his client had done could really not have been his fault.

"Hey, no way were you responsible," said one of the older members of our group. "Suicide is like a heart attack, except it's mental—There were probably lots of reasons—like even family stuff-- over a long period of time. Stop kicking yourself. Can't be your fault!"

During the discussion that followed, John said he had continued to work with the boy and his family following the suicide attempt, but he had still not resolved his own feelings of responsibility and guilt. John's experience frightened us, including some who also worried about the negative impact a client's suicide might have on their practice.

A year later, unfortunately, I had a similar experience which I found profoundly upsetting. I had been working with a teen-age girl who was depressed. Initially I thought her behavior was more schizoid than suicidal, but when Terry became more depressed despite my efforts to help her, I really got worried and suggested to her parents that we ought to obtain a psychiatric consultation to see if medication might be helpful. I was very frustrated, because Terry's parents, who were Christian Scientists, rejected the idea of her seeing a psychiatrist and they absolutely refused to consider any sort of medication.

"We do not believe in prescription medication under any circumstances!" they said. "It's against what we believe. Terry's fate is in God's hands," they insisted. "Our prayers will get her through! Besides",they continued," isn't this just a stage all adolescents go through?" For a moment or two, I couldn't say anything. I was angry. Their refusal to get the help I thought Terry needed, because of their religious views, was simply unacceptable to my way of thinking. But then I realized that what they were saying was really a kind of denial. I had to deal with that.

"No, I don't think so," I told them." Terry looks more troubled than most kids. The angry outbursts at home you've told me about, and the depth of depression we've both seen, really worries me!"

"Are you implying that our faith in prayer won't be enough?" her mother asked. "Yes, I am," I said. "You've asked me that before, and now that I've gotten to know her it's my opinion that Terry also needs medical help. I've listened to her—a lot about what troubles her. If we can get her on meds, along with my continuing to work with her, it could really be effective. But, without medication, I don't think I can accomplish much more than we have already."

"Are you saying you won't work with her anymore?" she asked. "No, not at all. I'm not saying that," I replied. "We're working well together, and I think she trusts me. But her mood swings are uncontrollable. I just think she needs meds to moderate the highs and lows enough so I can help her control them better. Isn't it worth a try?"

Terry's parents continued to refuse medication. I worked with her a short while longer, but they soon found a counselor within their church who agreed with their views. At our last session, Terry simply shrugged. "It's what they want," she said; "besides, I don't think I have any choice." It was a situation I felt I couldn't do anything about, but I tried any way. I called Terry's parents again and reiterated what I felt Terry needed, but I got nowhere.

Then, a little less than a year later, I was horrified to learn that Terry had committed suicide. While on a church youth-group trip to the Jersey shore, she had excused herself from one of the scheduled activities, and had gone over to the beach and into the rough surf. She had drowned before anyone could get to her. Onlookers said she just walked into the water, looking straight ahead, ignoring those who called to her, and wasn't seen again until the lifeguards dragged her body ashore.

I took the news of Terry's death very hard. I blamed myself for not having been able to convince her parents to pursue medical help. Then I received a letter from them expressing their sorrow, and thanking me for my efforts. The letter said that, unfortunately, what I had recommended was unacceptable, given their religious convictions, but that they appreciated my work with Terry. They also said they wanted to reassure me that their daughter was now in God's hands.

To this day, I remain saddened whenever I think about Terry's suicide. I keep wondering whether I should have persisted in trying to convince her parents to obtain the psychiatric help I thought she needed. That question still haunts me, even though I realize the situation was out of my hands after they decided to have Terry work with someone else. I had no control over the outcome after that.

I have also come to realize that, indeed, therapists have very limited control over many of the conditions surrounding the work we do with our clients. But, still, I wonder…

JUST LIKE MIKE

"So, what you been into?" asked Mike. "PCB's – smack – what?"

"Psychology," I laughed. "That's my field. I'm a psychologist."

"Wow – okay, man. That's cool. I can dig it. At least you're not pushing that crap about being into life," he smirked. "That's bullshit man."

It was the first meeting of our group, a newly-formed support group sponsored by "Genesis" a self-help center which I had helped organize to combat substance abuse in our community. It was the spring of 1970, and there was growing concern in several Fairfield County towns that too many of our adolescents and young adults were getting "hung up" on drugs. Several community self-help centers had spring up in a few of the towns, modeled after various "concept" anti-substance abuse approaches like Syanon, Renaissance, or Daytop, as well as 12- step programs like Alcoholics Anonymous. For the most part, the encounter groups in those programs were staffed by ex-addicts or former substance abusers who'd "been there" and could draw upon their personal experience to actively confront those "users" who had come seeking help. So Mike's question to me, the designated leader of our group, was understandable. He was checking me out.

"I don't have a drug problem, Mike. But I've had a lot of experience with people who do. I've also conducted different kinds of groups, including encounter groups before, so I think I can get us going and then maybe we can help one another, okay? Anything else you want to know about me?"

"No man, sounds cool. Let's move it," said Mike.

"Are you one of those shrinks that goes whooo-ooh?," asked Sally. She waved her hands, mimicking a magician casting a spell. Everyone laughed.

"No, I don't do mumbo jumbo, Sally." I faked astonishment, like she'd found me out. "That costs extra! No," I paused for emphasis, "I'm more a listener than a performer. And, learning to listen to one another, to better get to know one another, is something you'll hear me encourage you to do from time to time, when the people here try to tell us their stories.

We then went around the group as each member described a little bit about their problem with drugs and what they hoped the group might help them with. Each one of them expressed some feeling of desperation and loss of control, which they felt made it necessary to seek help. I sensed that most of them were sincere about seeking help. Although a few, like Mike, had probably come only because they had gotten into trouble with the police or some other authorities.

"I don't know if we're gonna be able to really help everyone here," I said. "But we're gonna try." I outlined the group's procedures, the limits of confidentiality, and the commitment we needed to make to listen and try to guide one another.

"Encounter is different from other groups you may have been in," I explained. "We try to be direct, upfront with one another. We don't have time to play 'head games.' You all know how easy it is to fall into the pit again, so we have to be tough with anyone who isn't serious about helping themselves. Only babies can't help themselves – you know the line."

"Yeah, I know it," said Arnie. "At Renaissance we had to wear signs that said, 'I'm a baby', around our necks. It was stupid shit, but it worked – for me at least, for a while anyway."

"So what happened? Why didn't you go back to Renaissance?" someone asked.

"I did three months in residence, but then went AWOL," Arnie answered. "I got into a fight with another resident and they blamed me for it. Then they threatened to take away my weekends, so I took off. But I couldn't hack it out on the street, so I'm here. I just can't go back to the house."

"Why not? They'll take you back," I asserted. "They'll give you some grief, but they'll take you back."

"I know." Arnie was staring at the floor. "I know – I just ain't there yet." He shook his head.

"Okay, we won't push you – yet. But you probably need to go back and finish the program. We'll work on it," I added.

Mike was nodding his head, like he agreed. So was Sheila, a short, stocky young woman, in her late twenties, who announced she was a lesbian, when we went around on introductions.

"You been in a program before?" someone asked her.

"Yeah, I know 'concept.' Daytop was like that. They make it tough on you, but it works. I was clean for two years."

"So, what happened?" I asked.

"You know the story." My partner walked out on me last summer while we were working in Provincetown. I was okay with that for a while, but then got in with some negative friends. Started 'shootin' up again, and then the holidays did me in. you know the story."

"Yeah, I think I do," I said. "But some of the folks here may not. And you were clean for a stretch, so maybe you can help out with some of the others who don't think that's possible?"

"You think so?" asked Sheila. "Yeah, I guess I can do that." She was smiling. The idea seemed to perk her up.

"C'mon, give me a break. She's a loser!" muttered Mike.

"That's a killer statement!" yelled Anita. "That shouldn't be allowed in here!"

"Give her a fuckin break, Mike! Maybe you'll learn something," Arnie pointed his finger at Mike, who looked like he wished he hadn't said anything.

"What I mean – I'm sorry Sheila –", Mike answered, "I didn't mean that the way it sounded –"

"So how did you mean it mother fucker?" Sheila was more angry than hurt. "You know how to bag someone don't you? Where'd you learn that, shithead?"

"No, really. I'm sorry. I said I was sorry, didn't I? I mean it – I'm sorry. It just came out wrong. What I meant was if you blew it, how can you help anyone else, man?"

I decided to step in at that point. Mike wasn't making things any better with his assertions, and Sheila was fuming.

"Sheila may have blown it by falling back in the hole, but that doesn't make her a loser," I said. Probably everyone here has failed more than once. She was clean for a two year stretch. That's worth something, isn't it? Maybe she learned something from it and maybe some of the rest of the group can too."

"Yeah," sighed Mike. "Yeah, maybe she can."

"What is your problem, shithead?" Sheila was too angry to let go. "Just what is your problem?" she persisted.

"It's not you," Mike feebly waved her off. "It's me. Like I can't believe anything anymore. I can't believe – and I don't trust no one!"

"Ahh, poor baby, what's your story, baby? Maybe you want a pacifier?" Arnie, who had defended Sheila a few moments earlier, was now on Mike's back.

"Back off, Arnie," I urged. "Let him tell his story."

What Mike told the group that day took up the rest of the meeting and left some of us, except Sheila who couldn't quite forgive him, staring at him in disbelief. The rest of us expressed amazement that Mike had survived what he told us he'd been through.

Mike, who was going on eighteen, said he was the only son of an affluent Greenwich family. His mother was a well-known author of children's books, and his father owned several automobile dealerships in Westchester County, just over the state line in New York. Mike's two older sisters were popular socialites. He, himself, had gone to an expensive private boarding school and it was expected that he would manage one of his father's dealerships upon graduation from college. But Mike had other ideas – rebellious, irresponsible ideas. He had been smart enough to get by on minimal effort in school, but he had also been suspended twice during his Junior year – once for possession of drugs, and once for dealing to other high- school students. His father's generous contributions to the school were all that kept him from being expelled. Finally, he was expelled just before graduation, for conducting a secret "midnight mass" in a nearby cemetery with a "coven" of his followers. That same night, his cult-group desecrated several graves. His father kept it out of the newspapers, but only for a while. Mike told us he truly believed he was a disciple of Satan, and had behaved accordingly by conducting ritual services to invoke the Devil's guidance. He also encouraged others to follow the dictates of

Satan, and he learned to speak in "tongues" or "glossolalia," which involved making unintelligible speech-like sounds designed to give the appearance of his having deep mysterious religious powers. Mike told us he tried to convey the impression that he was a "healer," until one night a group of disenchanted followers beat up on him pretty badly, and nearly blinded him in one eye. His father paid all his hospital bills, of course, but once Mike regained most of his strength, his father disowned him and threw him out of his house. Mike's father later renounced him as a total disgrace to the family and told Mike he would never again receive support from him. Mike said that as he walked out of the house, his father screamed at him, "You can go to Hell! I don't ever want to see you again. As far as we're concerned, you're dead!"

Mike's story unfolded further. He roamed New York City streets for a few months, fell prey to the dealers for whom he'd once helped distribute drugs, and even worked briefly for one of them as a male prostitute to support his habit. Finally, he said he had the good sense to get out of the city when one of his old classmates, who he had met by chance at a McDonald's, offered him a place to stay in White Plains. He described how he then entered a detoxification program in a Westchester hospital, "cleaned himself up," and got his job back, in Connecticut, in an automotive repair shop run by the uncle of one of his old school buddies. He found out about Genesis through one of the shop repairmen, and decided to see if we could help him stay off drugs.

"But I don't know," said Mike. "As soon as people get to know me they begin to hate me. And then I am likely to be betrayed, like when I was doing tongues." He smiled, his eyes swept around our circle. He pointed at Sheila. "And now, dear Sheila," he stared at her, "I've achieved your eternal love as well, haven't I?"

"Fuck off!" said Sheila with a shrug. Mike's story had diminished her annoyance with him, and she had obviously become a bit concerned. We all felt concerned about him. If his story was to be believed, it had successfully elicited sympathy among most of the group members and there seemed to be genuine interest in trying to help him. Nevertheless, there was a touch of sarcasm in his last comment to Sheila, and that worried me. He had seemed a bit too glib. Perhaps he was being manipulative. I thought there was something suggestive of the kind of storytelling one tends to associate with charismatic satanic- cult leaders and faith healers.

Unfortunately, my concerns about Mike were borne out during subsequent group meetings. His huge intellect and fund of knowledge continued to impress us. He told more seemingly incredible stories about his private school experiences and his troubled life in New York City. At times, he seemed insightful and seemingly helpful when other group members described their problems. Sometimes Sally and even Arnie or Sheila, would pick up on a comment Mike made, or an insight he expressed about someone else in the group.

"You know, it's just like what Mike just said," I once heard Arnie say.

"Yeah, Mike's right," one of the others said, and Mike's smile suggested satisfaction over how others seemed to follow his lead.

Despite my reservations about his sincerity, I encouraged him. I felt a bit apprehensive about reinforcing his emerging leadership role in the group, because I worried that he might use it to manipulate others, but that didn't happen, at least not to my knowledge. Even though he was the youngest in the group, most of them respected his "street smarts," as well as his ability to articulate deep concern for others. They also came to value his practical suggestions about how to deal with others in family matters, based upon what he felt had alienated him from his own family, even though it was clear that he still very much resented his father. He made such good sense in his advice to others that the group began tossing his advice back at him. For example, they told him he ought to seriously consider calling his father and try to reconcile matters with his family. Mike couldn't duck it. He said he would think about it.

Two months later, just before the group was getting ready for our break, Mike told us he'd made an important decision. He announced that he had telephoned his father and made a lunch date. He said he was feeling anxious about the whole idea, but would "do the lunch – no matter what."

I got a call from him a week later. Mike said the luncheon went well. He added with a touch of sarcasm in his voice that "All was forgiven," and that he was "back on track toward inheriting family wealth and obtaining happiness." But none of us ever heard from him again, until some years later, when a colleague of mine informed me that he thought he'd read an article somewhere that Mike had committed suicide. My colleague remembered that Mike had come from a wealthy family and that the newspaper article had described how the family was grieving for him and couldn't understand why he would want to commit suicide.

"No," I said, "that's not like our Mike. He would never have let things get to him to the extent that he might commit suicide."

Indeed, several years later I learned that Mike was still alive, that he was well, and had joined the priesthood of a proselytizing religious order.

"That's more like it," I thought. "That's just like Mike!"

BACK ON TRACK

Ellis and Marilyn had been married for 45 years. Ellis had recently retired from the engineering firm he had started years earlier and was searching for things to do around the house to keep busy. Meanwhile, Marilyn continued to enjoy her employment as a real estate broker. But Ellis' searching to keep himself busy wasn't the problem. Their grown children had married, had established families of their own in places nearby enough to visit occasionally, but far enough away to limit meddling. So the children weren't the problem either. Nor was the problem the fact that Marilyn's hours were erratic and that she had to spend some weekend time with house hunting clients. They said they actually had a lot of time to spend together, and that <u>that</u> was the problem! It was not so much that they needed to spend more or less time together, but that the time they did spend together was either boring or unsatisfying – "like after all these years, somehow we have really lost touch with one another. In fact, it feels like we're constantly irritating one another in a million countless ways."

Ellis and Marilyn therefore came into counseling asking if they ought to separate for a while and see if that might rekindle the loving and caring they once shared. They even wondered if "maybe we just ought to split and go our separate ways. That would really be something!" Marilyn commented. "Most of our friends consider us to be Fairfield County's ideal, long-time married couple." "Yeah," added Ellis, "we've really gone sour."

Listening to them go on about all they felt they'd lost and, more importantly, what they once had, it became clear that separating was not what either of them really wanted. They had invested a lot in each other and their kids. So I urged them to look at all they'd accomplished together, and what they'd come to learn about each other over the years. For example, I had them draw up lists about what they felt they'd gained just from knowing each other, and, also, what they felt they'd learned about each other through parenting their kids together. Making those lists was posed as a form of homework assignment, and they liked the idea. Then, we examined the lists they brought in, and we devoted several sessions to discussing the various reasons why they had lost sight of those positive attributes.

The use of homework assignments, to detail what had been enjoyable earlier in their relationship, is derived from Eric Fromm's writing about the main factors in a loving relationship, but the homework procedures have been developed by cognitive-behaviorally oriented psychologists. For Ellis and Marilyn, aided by the process of reviewing the many good years they had shared in their marriage, the homework approach proved most helpful. Their more recent difficulties arose from issues which many adult couples experience. Ellis had lost his identity as a hard working, enterprising engineer; he missed his former colleagues and business associates. He was not yet comfortable with retirement and had not yet replaced his lost career-defined self with anything satisfactory. He was enjoying some of the leisure activities he had longed for during his pre-retirement years, but he had lost a sense of purpose. Initially, Marilyn had enjoyed having Ellis around the house more, but then she gradually found him "underfoot" too much and was irritated by his having become bothersome and demanding. She had also become impatient with his restlessness, and generally gloomy outlook. She wanted to push him to "get off his butt and get busy," but Ellis perceived her pushing as criticism and insensitivity. They had indeed begun spinning away from one another.

Together, after a careful exploration of what was good in their earlier relationship and how their difficulties had evolved, we devised some fairly simple courses of action to try. They themselves suggested a number of small, almost inconsequential things each might do for the other. They were things they knew would please the other, but that they had stopped doing. We, therefore, developed separate lists for each of them – of acceptable and doable activities which they could employ, whenever they chose to. The activities were relative to their available time together and incorporated their shared interests. We then monitored the perceived outcome of those activities over a prescribed period of time. Even though some of the chosen activities appeared superficial and mundane, the desired effect was quickly apparent. Gradually, Ellis perceived Marilyn as less critical toward him and generally supportive of his needs, while Marilyn began to feel that they were talking and generally enjoying more of their time together again. Finally, we discussed what actually had changed, and agreed to a series of periodic checkups. We ended our sessions a few months later, optimistic that, although the issues which had been driving them apart might recur, they were likely to be more readily solvable. They said they were essentially "back on track", but would keep their "activity lists handy just in case!"

MEMORIES

During the years I conducted retirement support groups, I found that the oldest members had the least difficulty reporting their life experiences. Some were initially reluctant to tell their stories in any great detail, usually because of all they claimed they had long since forgotten, but when questioned by other members of the group, or urged to dredge up anything they might recollect, they generally responded with enthusiasm. As a result, hazy remembrances were often retrieved and colorfully embellished, to the enjoyment of us all, as if we had been rewarded for our persistent probing for what the tale-teller had to say.

Martin Duvalier, who had recently joined one such group, had earlier dropped the hint that he came from a line of professional prizefighters and might be pleased to tell the group about it if they were interested. No one took him up on it right away, but one of the other group members, who had had some boxing experience, suggested later on in the meeting that we let Martin tell his story. Martin needed little further encouragement.

"I am the grandson of the great Battling Dante Duvalier," he announced. His French accent was very noticeable. "My grandfather was the pride of Versailles – having fought his way to the light heavyweight championship of Europe during the years following World War I."

Martin went on for nearly twenty minutes, describing how proud his family was of his grandfather's accomplishments in the ring. Interestingly, his accent continued to become more and more exaggerated as he spoke.

"Grandpere Dante was, in fact, considered to be the top contender for the World's Heavyweight Crown worn by Jack Dempsey during the early 1920's," he continued. "And he would have fought Dempsey for the title, but Dempsey's handlers claimed he was fifteen pounds under the weight limit and therefore couldn't qualify as a bona fide challenger. That, of course, was nonsense! They were frightened of him, his speed, his quickness, his powerful right hand. He could have easily gained the necessary pounds to meet their weight limit. Most certainly, he would have beaten the great Dempsey into a pulp. All of France remembers that Dante should have been the Heavyweight Champion of the world."

Someone asked, "What about you Martin? Or your father? Either of you follow in your grandfather's footsteps?"

Martin shrugged. "No. My father was an accountant. He never took up boxing. He idolized his father, but I think he never felt he could match his greatness. And I, well that's another story. I fought a little in college and had a few amateur fights afterward, but I lacked my grandfather's quickness and my arms were too short. I was TKO'd in my last bout and I guess that was it.. I became an accountant like my father and never fought again. But you know what – everyone remembers my grandfather. Our Battling Dante – he was something. Everyone in our family knows he could have been champion of the world! I will always remember that!"

Jeannie Thompson, another member of our support group, needed much more encouragement to tell her story. She had once commented that she'd been a pretty good dancer as a young woman, but it wasn't until many sessions later that we were all amazed to learn how much more there was to her experience on the dance floor. Jeannie had actually been a "hoofer." She had even danced professionally as one of the original Ziegfeld Follies girls. Our quiet, understated Jeannie Thompson, whose stage name we learned was Jan Austin, when she was in the Follies, later became Jean Thompson after she had married (while she was then performing with the famous June Taylor dancers). Jeannie then gradually revealed more about having almost become more of a stage celebrity.

It seems that she had never fully gained "star" status with either Ziegfeld or June Taylor. Like Martin's brief career in boxing, she had enjoyed her chorus line notoriety and a few glittery moments in the limelight, but she chose to pursue the more sedate life of a ballroom dance instructor, while starting her family with Mr. Thompson, a successful construction engineer. Joe Thompson, the stereotypical "stage-door Johnnie" had actually wooed her while she was still dancing in the Follies and he later was very supportive about her continuing to dance professionally, but he finally convinced Jeannie that raising their kids was likely to be more rewarding in the long run than the fleeting excitement of life upon the stage.

"We still went dancing as often as we could," said Jeannie. "Joe was an excellent dancer, not your plodding, always stepping-on-your-toes type, so it's not like I ever gave up entirely on my dancing. And after the kids went off to school, I did some dance classes at the Y and gave private ballroom instruction for several years until my hip went out and I had to give it up."

"Do you miss it?" I asked.

"No, not really," Jeannie considered. "Stardom had evaded me, but I did continue dancing, still do, in fact, even though I can't do most of what I used to do. And, though Joe passed away several years ago, I've still got my kids and they're terrific kids. Who knows who or what I'd have today if I stayed on the stage."

"Sounds like you have no regrets," someone said.

"Oh no, not at all. Like I said, I've had a good life and still have my family. I miss Joe not being around, but life goes on, and ..." Jeannie paused. She slipped back into her characteristic quietness.

"And what?" I urged.

"And I too have lots of memories," she said.

I'VE GOT YOU BABE

Gerry and Karen walked into my office, sat down as far apart as possible on the couch, and immediately began screaming at each other.

"You son of a bitch! What do you mean you don't want me to work? Where do you come off dictating whether or not I can work?" Karen's voice was shrill and getting louder.

Gerry turned to me to cue me in that this was a fight that they'd begun in their car on the way to today's appointment, His face was flushed. He turned back to Karen and pointed his finger at her.

"Now you listen to me. I don't care if you've got a million job offers; you are not going to leave our kids to be raised by a God-Damn Nanny -- not my kids!"

"Then *you* take care of them, shithead! Someone around here has got to work. You've done nothing since you were laid off, but sit on your ass and complain. I've had it with you!"

"Karen," Gerry's voice was softer. He shifted to a more conciliatory tone. "Look, we came here to work things out, right? Okay, I got laid off. I didn't expect it and it's got me down, But I've got 6 months separation left, plus continued benefits and I'm starting to look. Give me a fuckin' break already! I'm starting to look."

Karen seemed unimpressed, but she'd calmed down. "I've heard that bullshit before, Gerry. You keep saying you're ready to start job hunting, but you still can't get out of bed in the morning. What do you mean you're starting to look? At what? The TV? Who are you kidding?"

"I called Morgan yesterday," said Gerry, "He's got a lead for me. VP in a publishing house. What the hell, he hunted me didn't he when I got my last job."

"Gerry, you're kidding yourself," Karen answered. "Morgan knows how depressed you've been. He's throwing you a bone to keep you afloat. You can't count on him. You've got to get out and make your own leads."

"Karen's right," I intervened. "Listening to the two of you go at each other has made a few things clear. Gerry, you're wanting to start looking sounds to me like the medicine we got prescribed for you, is beginning to kick in. And you know the publishing business better than anyone does. But you've got to call around and make the contacts yourself. You know that, that's also clear, but my question is, are you up for it? Do you feel like you can hack it out there?"

Gerry hesitated. Then leaned forward. "Well, yes. I think I'm ready," he said. "But when Karen gives me grief, it throws me."

"Ah, poor baby – so it's my fault again if you run back to bed. Give me a break!" Karen, who until recently had desperately tried consoling and cajoling to get Gerry moving again had become so impatient with him that, as I listened to her, it was evident that Gerry's beginning to show more signs of life hadn't yet impressed her. She was still anxious for him to get out from underfoot and resume the wage- earner role she and their two kids had previously depended on. My job was to help them navigate the slow path back from his depression.

Gerry and Karen had been married for more than 15 years. He had been an extremely successful executive in a major book publishing company, but he lost out when a merger eliminated his position, He was actually fired by someone he'd hired several years earlier, who had become the company CEO. Gerry was, therefore, surprised, extremely upset, and embittered by the unexpected chain of events which led to his dismissal. He had received a decent buyout, considering all the years he had worked to develop the company, but having been let go, under the circumstances he'd described to me, his subsequent depression was not surprising. Karen and he, up until then, had been enjoying all the trappings of an affluent suburban life. She had left her job, as a highly paid executive secretary in an advertising firm, to raise their young children, and was, therefore, resentful that Gerry was taking so long to get going again.

"After all," Karen continued, "he doesn't *look* sick. He just lies around the house like an immovable lump and it aggravates me that it's taking him so long to make any moves to help us. It took him three whole months to finally admit he was depressed, and then it took another month before he had the guts to call you for an appointment."

"But, he finally *did* call, Karen," I said, "and that's a tough first move for anyone struggling with depression. I can tell you about it firsthand, Karen. I went through my own depression several years ago and I drove my wife wild about it at first, not wanting to talk about it to anyone, and then taking a while longer to be willing to call a therapist for an appointment. I know how hard it is, Karen, to make those first moves. But when you do come through it finally, you feel stronger than you've ever felt before. It just takes time to build back your confidence – to feel competent again, instead of feeling worthless, or that you can't do anything to help yourself."

"Well, I'll take your word for it, Doc," Karen said. "Maybe I am being impatient, but he's been a pain in the ass now for a long time!"

"See, there she goes again," Gerry muttered. "You tell her like it is, and in a few seconds she's on my back again. It's no win. I start to feel better, slip back, and she's all over me again."

"You can't really blame her, Gerry," I interrupted. "What she had to put up with you when you couldn't even get out of bed, is crazy making – especially when she's worried over what will happen to her and the kids if you can't get through it. It's very scary for her.

"Okay, so what's next?" said Gerry. "Where do we go from here?"

"It's where do *you* go from here, Gerry," I replied," Making that first bunch of calls to the outside world is the most difficult. Why not work with Karen on it; use her business skills, set up a schedule of who to call and when to call, and then let Karen call ahead to schedule your appointments with whoever you can get to see. Then push yourself to meet your schedule. It will seem overwhelming at first, but you know a lot about the business. You've been successful at it for so many years, better than most I suspect, so you have to get your ass in gear, force yourself to keep one foot going in front of the other, and like the 'ad' people say 'do it!'"

"Easy for you to say, Doc,"said Gerry.

"Maybe Gerry," I answered, "But you're looking at someone who also had a hard time getting going. Anyway, I managed to do it. So I know you can do it. It's the getting started part that's most difficult, and I know Karen will help – even if she is fed up with where you've been."

Karen was smiling. "You better believe it, Gerry. You get me crazy when you won't help yourself, but I'm here for you. I'll do all I can to help you get started again – just try me –."

Gerry sat up straight, nodding. Then he looked at me and smiled at Karen, as she moved closer to his side of the couch.

"Hey Karen," I said. "It's like that old Sonny and Cher song. You know, the one that made them so popular when they had their first TV show – the one they sang together, 'I've got you Babe!'"

Karen hugged Gerry and they got up and left my office. I still had my doubts that Gerry would be up for what we'd discussed, but it was clear that he was on his way, and it was equally clear, by validating Karen's frustrations with him, that she might now be able to be a bit more patient and willing to help him with his first baby steps out of his depression. I felt hopeful that he would succeed.

Gerry did succeed. At least he began making calls to old contacts, got a few leads and actually went for a couple of interviews. When they showed for their appointment two weeks later, there was no screaming, no angry accusations, no remonstrating. They walked into my office, huddled together on the couch and announced that they were ready to discontinue treatment. Karen was beaming.

"I know I've still got a long way to go to pull out of my depression," said Gerry, "but I feel like I'm off and running. I actually found myself singing while driving to a job interview. I haven't done that in over a whole year."

I gave a purposefully professional "uh hum."

"You don't believe him, do you?" Karen laughed.

"No, it's not that I don't believe him, Karen." I said. "I do. In fact, what he's describing is how I felt while I began getting over my own depression. I was riding along in my car, and also suddenly found myself singing."

"But you seem a little pessimistic," said Gerry.

"Not at all Gerry," I said. "I'm really glad to see you feeling up."

"So why not join in our fun?" said Karen, smiling. "In fact, we're thinking of discontinuing. But," she added, "We intend to send you your fee for a few months just to keep our account open."

It was my turn to laugh. "No, Gerry, send me no fees – I will manage – somehow."

"So what is it, then?" asked Karen.

"Just this. I want you guys to be aware that the road back may still have ruts in it. You're in for at least a few times when you're gonna be feeling apprehensive again – that the big hole is beckoning again. Everyone has that experience after they've come out of a depression. You just have to be prepared for it, that's all, and it won't be too difficult to get through, especially Gerry, if you keep taking your medication. Too many people, once they're feeling good again, make the mistake of quitting their meds too soon. Don't you do it."

"Thanks for the warning, coach. I really appreciate you saying that," said Gerry. "Falling down again *is* what I most worry about."

We talked a while more about what to expect during post-depression, and then they got up to leave, arm in arm, still joking about paying on their account whether or not they returned.

"Okay, excellent idea," I said, just as they were walking out, "I'll keep your money in escrow, and what *you* can do is deposit some money in your own bank account every time you have a fight or start screaming again at each other."

"We will," they said. "We will!"

Exactly one year later, I received a postcard from Gerry and Karen. They were in Aruba on vacation. The card said ... "We're enjoying ourselves immensely. Visa air-miles plus our screaming-therapy account bought us our time here in the sun. Wish you were here. No, we take that back. Please cancel the escrow account. Your services are no longer needed."

FORGETFULNESS, POOR HEARING, AND SEX

Earlier, Merrill had announced that he couldn't find his hearing aid, "Maybe I left it at home," he said. Then turning to me, he asked if I might speak a little louder today. Bertha, who also used an aid, nodded agreement so I mouthed, without sound, "Of course, Merrill, is this loud enough?"

"What," responded Merrill, leaning forward, cupping his hand over his left ear, a perplexed look spreading across his large, lantern-jawed face.

Again, I mouthed, "Is this better, Merrill?" exaggerating my lip movements, but still making no sound.

Sarah, seated next to Merrill, doubled over in a fit of laughter. Loud guffaws and snickering from the back rows filled the room. "That will teach you to forget your hearing aid, Merrill," shouted Helen, who was seated near the door.

Merrill's moment of perplexity was followed by a look of astonishment when he heard all the laughing and everyone seeming to make fun of him, but then he caught on and joined in the hilarity, acknowledging that the joke was on him. He even held his hands up, turned, waved his cap in the air as if acknowledging applause for some heroic feat and sat back in his seat, nodding good naturedly, smiling that I'd put one over on him.

I knew Merrill would not be embarrassed. On the contrary, he seemed delighted with all that had happened. He often invited others' kidding him about his obvious physical limitations. In fact, he usually was the one to instigate similar pranks among the regulars at the Senior Center.

Our group met every Tuesday afternoon to talk about everything and anything of current interest, to discuss recent news events, concerns about aging, or any question anyone might have regarding my knowledge of the field of psychology. Usually anywhere from fifteen to twenty-five of the Center's regulars (ranging in age from 70 to 95) were in attendance, most having just finished their lunch in the cafeteria. That, of course, meant that a fair amount of nodding off, even snoring, had to be tolerated as long as it wasn't too loud or disruptive.

"Nudge him," I might say when someone's sonorous snores and loud gulping for air became too distracting. No one seemed to mind being awakened that way because it occurred fairly frequently. And after five years of conducting our weekly meetings right after lunchtime, I no longer took it personally or felt that it was me who put anyone to sleep.

A few moments later, having just gotten into a discussion on dream analysis, after Margaret asked if I ever interpreted clients' dreams, Merrill announced with a grand gesture to all that he'd found his hearing aid. He ceremoniously plunked it into his ear canal and said, "Now, say anything you want, Doc, I'm all ears!"

"I was just saying Merrill that ears often show up in dreams as having important symbolic significance."

"What," said Merrill, looking perplexed again.

"Yes," I continued. "Since early Egyptian times, ears have symbolized heightened awareness, particularly deep apprehensiveness."

"What?" Merrill's deeply furrowed brow now added to his look of perplexity. "Egyptian what, what are you talking about?"

Sheila, from her back row seat piped in, "He's saying that dreaming about ears has important symbolic meaning."

Merrill, turning in his seat to face Sheila, answered "Dreaming about ears? Who the hell ever dreams about ears?"

"No one," I stated. "It's extremely uncommon."

When everyone laughed, Merrill slumped down in his seat, his hands covering his face in mock despair. He then signaled with upraised, clenched fist that he'd been had again.

I shook my head. "Merrill, that's twice in 10 minutes."

"Some days are like that," he nodded, pulling his baseball cap down over his ears. "Go ahead -- I'll be good."

Merrill was one of my favorites of the regulars in the group. Always responsive, often clowning, I could always count on Merrill to liven any discussion. And he was, despite moments of forgetfulness or word finding difficulty, most often articulate and extremely knowledgeable. Therefore, everyone readily tolerated his antics, warmly enjoyed his pranks, and quickly consoled him when he expressed genuine concern about his occasional forgetting or confusion. Our openly discussing *that* most common symptom of aging, which all of us shared, was one of the nice, reassuring aspects of our weekly meetings.

I continued on about the basics of dream interpretation in therapy without further mention of the meaning of ears. Almost everyone had something to say because dreaming, they agreed, is so common an experience, even when you forget whatever it was you dreamed.

Elliot, in fact, complained that he knew he dreamed a lot, but he never remembered anything about any of his dreams. Martha, his wife, almost always seated at his side, poked him, "I can verify that he does a lot of dreaming because he talks in his sleep. And," she added with a smile, "some of what he says can get embarrassing."

"I only dream about you, dear," Elliot retorted, obviously pleased with Martha's hinting about his sexual prowess.

"I thought you just said you can't remember any of your dreams," she playfully nudged him again.

"Oh, but when they're about you, I always remember," answered Elliot.

"You're a liar, but I still love you," Martha retorted, affectionately patting his shoulder. The group nodded. They often regarded the couple's obvious fondness for one another with a touch of sarcastic envy.

"Dreams are often sexy," I reflected, "especially when you're young. Has something to do with active hormones and all that youthful sexual energy -- as well as those unmentionable hidden desires." I paused for effect and looked around. Most of them were smiling. "Seriously," I added, "dreaming is really how the body responds to whatever is left over, the residue from the day's excitement, sexual or otherwise. It's the body's way of staying asleep when something internal or external actively stimulates any sort of arousal. For example," I explained, "the sleeping body's response to the need to relieve one's bladder, can actually produce dreams about going to the bathroom, before the increasing need to pee wakes you up."

"What's peeing got to do with sex?" asked Harold, disappointed that we seemed to be getting off the point.

"Only that all persistent bodily functions stimulate dreaming. Just like an open window blowing cold air into your bedroom can arouse dreaming about walking through the snow," I explained.

"Let's go back to the sex," said Harold, leering at Anita across the room. She batted her eyelids in mock demureness and everyone laughed.

"OK, back to dreams about sex," I said. "Anyone remember any sort of sex dream?"

The group was silent.

"Harold, I'm disappointed. I thought you'd be first." Harold just shrugged.

Finally, Marcia tentatively raised her hand. "Well, I'll tell one," she asserted. "But the problem is, in all my sexy dreams, whoever I'm making love with, has no face."

"That's because there's a kind of dream-censor that gives certain sex dreams an X rating."

"What!" she exclaimed, "You mean like how movies are rated?"

"Yeah, remember we said that dreaming is intended to keep you asleep. It's because of the body's need to continue regenerating itself while you're at rest. So if your sex glands are operating on high drive, the dream is distorted by a central executive signal or censoring process which alleviates any arousal of anxiety that might, in turn, be disturbing enough to wake you up. In other words, if you saw the face of your lover it might not be someone you wanted to have sex with, hence the face is a blank."

"Oh, oh!" Marcia exclaimed, then she looked over to Phil who had turned and was wagging his finger at her as if playfully warning her to say no more.

"What are you getting all excited about Mosley? It would never be you!" she laughed.

"That's the point Marcia," I interjected. "The dream censor keeps Phil's or anyone else's face out of your dream so you can keep enjoying whatever you're doing in your dream. If Phil's face actually appeared, it could be so agitating it might wake you up."

"Hey, wait a minute," yelled Phil. "I'm not sure I appreciate this -- in fact, I'm feeling downright insulted!"

We spent the next few minutes cajoling Phil out of his feigned distress. It was obvious that he enjoyed the special attention.

"What about dreams that *do* wake you up?" asked Terry. "You know, like if someone's chasing you and you can't move -- and you wake up in a sweat?"

"Good question, Terry. That's called an anxiety dream, one that reflects stuff from the previous day which is still unresolved or troubling you. The dream censor can't deal with it, so you wake up often with a start, feeling agitated and upset. But we've just run out of time, so if it's okay with you, Terry, let's pick up with that next week. Meanwhile, everyone write down your dreams if you can remember them, and we'll see if they have any special meaning."

As everyone got up to leave, Raymond, who had been noticeably nodding on and off most of the session called out, "Hey, Doc, next week, can we talk about sex dreams?"

CALL ME RAYMOND

We met several years ago at a Senior Center luncheon. Raymond Vargas clearly stood out in both his manner and appearance. He was quite tall, more than six feet, broad chested but not overweight, and slightly stooped over from more than 70 years of life's wear and tear. His large, roundish face was darkly pouched, with deep eye-sockets. He actually conveyed an imposing, almost menacing impression. I was reminded a little of Orson Welles, the corrupt police chief in "A Touch of Evil."

I also quickly learned that Raymond Vargas tolerated no nicknames. I had turned to shake his hand after the round of introductions at our table.

I said, "Ray, I --"

He interrupted me. His hand shot up like a traffic cop. "It's not Ray!" he boomed and then ruffled, "My name is Raymond, not Ray, not Raymie, nor any other diminutive you might expect me to readily answer to."

"You know you just split an infinitive," I said, smiling through my momentary embarrassment.

Raymond laughed out loud -- rather, he bellowed. "What did you say? I split a what?"

"An infinitive, it's a grammatical figure of speech," I answered.

"That's what I thought you said. I know what a split infinitive is. I'm retired, but I'm also a writer. It's just that I didn't expect to hear you say what you just said." Raymond's voice lowered a bit. "Perhaps I was being a bit stuffy, but I hate when someone who doesn't know you presumes --"

"No," I shook my head, "My fault -- I did presume -- you have every right to be a Raymond."

"Wait a minute," he answered, his voice rising again. Then he smiled, "I'm not exactly sure how you meant that!"

Raymond and I enjoyed the luncheon. As we talked, we found that we enjoyed many similar interests. We also discovered that we each had hearing difficulties which, I thought to myself, probably accounted for his overly loud voice.

Raymond leaned toward me, his face serious. A few wisps of gray hair broke the smooth contour of his otherwise bald head.

"You know I actually think I scare people away. They tell me to stop shouting at them. I join a group engaged in pleasant conversation, and within a few moments they begin to leave. Do *you* think I'm too loud?"

"What," I said.

"C'mon," he said, "Tell me the truth. Really, do you think I'm too loud?"

"Yes."

"No --"

"Yes," I repeated. "It's probably because you have more than usual hearing loss for someone your age. Have you ever had your ears checked? If not, I know a place where you can go."

"Maria Ouspenskaya, that's it. In 'The Wolfman.' Remember, she says that to Talbot when he tells her he needs to get help -- she says, in that raspy little voice of hers, 'I know a place where we can go.'" Raymond's Transylvanian accent was almost perfect.

"You really *don't* want to get your hearing checked, do you?" I persisted.

"Once again, you presume," he said. "But quite frankly," he said. "I don't think I want to know how much of it I've lost."

Raymond and I talked awhile longer after lunch, about things having to do with hearing loss, and the related problems we both had experienced. Then he surprised me. He said he knew I was a psychologist, asked for my card, and said he might like to come in and see me on a professional basis.

"I've got a few other problems -- a few personal questions," he said. "Maybe I can pick your brains for some answers?"

When Raymond came in for his appointment, I didn't quite know what to expect. He seemed uneasy, his big head teetering atop his totem-pole frame, he shifted about trying to find a comfortable position on my office couch. Finally, he began by referring again to his too-loud voice.

"Not only does my loud voice send people scurrying away," he muttered, "but it's created other problems for me too."

"Like what?" I asked.

"Well, like I've always been active in politics and I --"

"What party?" I asked.

"Uh, Republican - I'm on the Republican Town Committee. Why do you ask?" he said.

"My fees just doubled," I said, as straightfaced as possible.

"Why?" he laughed. "Do you dislike Republicans?"

"No," I answered. "They're just harder to cure."

We joked a bit about politics. I told Raymond I was an ardent Democrat, and acted insulted when he needled me about our being "somewhere to the left of Karl Marx." After a few more moments, bantering about local political issues, he seemed more relaxed. In fact, Raymond told me he had actually been interested in running for public office many years earlier, after he'd sold his engineering firm.

"But then my wife died after a long battle with lung cancer. I guess I lost interest in all that political nonsense." His voice lowered, "I lost interest in a lot of things when she died, politics, writing, friends -- we used to have so many friends --." I couldn't hear the rest of what he said. His voice had trailed off to a whisper.

Raymond said nothing for another moment or two. He seemed to be staring down at the rug under my cocktail table. When he looked up again, his face had reddened. He sat up straight. He seemed agitated. His voice rose.

"Now I have very few friends. No, let me restate that. Now I have absolutely *no* friends -- and do you know why?" Raymond roared, "because there are no people I like!"

I didn't respond, at least not immediately. I waited, then leaned forward, looking directly into his face. "You seem angry, Raymond. Would you like to tell me more about that?" I stated it slowly, in an exaggerated "Rogerian" manner.

Raymond roared again, "What!" Then he laughed out loud and banged his knee with the flat of his hand. "I've got to hand it to you," he said. "That takes the cake. Do you do that with all your patients?"

"Clients," I corrected him, "not patients -- it's a different kind of relationship. But, no, I decided to *not* take you seriously. You know -- about not liking anyone, because I don't think that's the problem."

"So what *is* the problem?" he asked. "If my not having any friends any more isn't the problem? What is?"

"Let's talk about your wife," I said.

It didn't take us long to get to the fact that Raymond was still grieving over his wife's death. They'd been married for nearly forty-five years, having met in college when both were in their early twenties. They had been unable to have children, despite many unsuccessful tries, but that fact actually created more closeness between them than most couples ordinarily experience.

"I miss her desperately," he said. "Still, after all those years. I don't think anyone could possibly replace her. No, no one could replace her!"

Raymond slammed his fist down on the cocktail table. "They just don't make people like her anymore," he added.

"Really," I said. "Well, if you believe that, the rest of us don't have much of a chance, do we?"

"What?" Raymond frowned. "Where did that come from?"

"Simple," I said. "How can anyone new you might ever meet, especially a woman, match up to your memory of your wife. You're a very loyal guy, Raymond."

"You're being sarcastic." He said.

"Maybe, a little I guess, but aren't you thinking you might be disloyal to her if you opened up to someone new? What would happen, do you think, if you met someone, an attractive woman, for example, and you started to like her?"

"I think I see what you mean."

"Well, then by extension, I think that holds you back from anyone you might otherwise let yourself get to like. It even gets you angry that it could happen."

"But, I like you -- and it even turns out that we're political enemies. How about that?"

"That's different." I answered, "but not entirely -- look what you did with me. You turned me into your therapist. Different from a close friend you can open up to when something, anything, is on your mind. You're not being disloyal, opening up to me, Raymond. Me you gotta pay."

Raymond just stared at me. Then a smile slowly crossed his face. "You know," he paused evidently for effect, "there's this woman I just met . . ."

We arranged no further appointments, but I did get a call from him a few weeks later asking for the name of the Center where I got my hearing checked and was fitted for the latest in hearing aids. After that when we ran into each other at the Senior Center (where I conducted my weekly discussion/support group) we'd often kid each other about our hearing problems, and I would ask him about whether he ever went for a hearing check. Raymond would simply turn on his big smile, shake his head and wag his finger at me. "You want to be on my most disliked list too?"

"Heavens, no!" I would reply. "Anything but that. "Then, "How's your new lady friend?" I asked.

"Mind your own business," said Raymond, his traffic cop's hand up again, but this time he was smiling broadly.

Several months later, I came across an announcement in our local newspaper. Raymond had become engaged to marry someone, who he told me later over the phone, "was a fine woman, of similar vintage, and like mind." He added that what we'd discussed, when we met in my office, had encouraged him to check out a local "Grieving" support group run by a colleague of mine at Norwalk Hospital. Raymond said that he had really gotten to know his bride-to-be, the woman he had mentioned to me at the end of our session together, after he had attended several group meetings.

He then said, "I'm glad we talked, you know, that time in your office. It gave me perspective. I even talked Carolyn, that's my fiancé, into going to some of the group meetings with me! She had also lost her husband to cancer."

Raymond died last spring. He had become ill while attending the Republican Presidential Nominating Convention as one of Connecticut's party representatives. He'd obviously resumed his active political interests. The local newspaper quoted his wife as saying that, although they had been married for only a few years, she "would particularly miss his sense of humor, his enthusiasm for doing new things, and -- even that loud voice of his, that people often complained about."

I guess he never went to get his hearing checked.

ON BEING AN
EXPERT WITNESS

Judge Alter stared over the top of her glasses, and leaned forward toward Dr. Martin. "So, when you use the term 'hype-reroticized,' what you mean is that this boy was easily sexually stimulated? And what you also apparently mean is that this 4 year old boy was exposed to provocative circumstances which got him upset, confused and somehow easily sexually aroused all at the same time – is that correct, Dr. Martin?"

"Yes, that's correct y

Your Honor." The psychiatrist looked directly up at the judge who continued to peer down from her bench.

"And, Dr. Martin, are you also saying that that experience has left a permanent scar on this little boy's psyche, so to speak, and that that experience might produce a poor psycho-sexual adjustment in the future?"

"Yes, Your Honor. That's what I fear may be in store for this young man as he gets older."

"Thank you, Dr. Martin. You may stand down – for now. I may have further questions."

The Honorable Judge Margaret Alter of the 7th District, in New York, was generally considered to be knowledgeable and fair by all who brought their cases before her in Family Relations Court. She had been a psychology major in her undergraduate days at Brooklyn College so she was considered to be fairly astute when it came to post-divorce custodial disputes involving allegations of child abuse or sexual molestation. She also knew that it was not uncommon for lawyers and their clients to litigate a sexual misconduct or abuse claim against an ex-spouse when the bottom-line issue was likely to be more about visitation or financial support matters. In addition, she knew that when she had expert psychiatric testimony presented to her in court regarding abuse allegations, she had to clearly ascertain what the possible long-term effect on the child's development might be. In other words, her job was to determine what might be in the child's future as well as his present "best interests."

Concerning Jimmy, now age 7, Dr. Martin's testimony supported Jimmy's mother (the plaintiff and primary custodian) in her claim that, when Jimmy was five, he said he had witnessed his father having sex with a woman (whom he later married) and that he had actually been encouraged to get into the shower with them afterwards. She said that from what Jimmy had told him, the experience was obviously traumatic and that she feared it might affect him for the rest of his life. She also suspected that there was probably some sexual molestation involved while they all showered together, and that Jimmy had seemed so upset by the incident, which took place at his father's home during a weekend visitation, that he had asked her many questions about sex and body parts over a long period of time. She had therefore requested a legal constraint on Jimmy's visitations with his father. That constraint was temporarily granted by the court pending an official hearing before Judge Alter.

I was asked by Jimmy's father and his lawyer to evaluate Jimmy regarding any alleged harm done as a result of the incident in question, and to testify in court afterward regarding my findings. I was also told to communicate what I found to the court-appointed advocate, an attorney representing Jimmy.

I found from my work with Jimmy that his relationship with his father was quite good and I detected no signs of earlier traumatic experience. I therefore had no hesitation about offering to testify in favor of maintaining the child's relationship with his father. I also had found nothing to suggest that the alleged shower incident or Jimmy's having observed his father and current wife in a sexual relationship could, in any way, have resulted in long-term negative effects on his development. I felt strongly, too, that the temporary restraining order on the father's visitation might be harmful to Jimmy who seemingly very much adored his father.

As the hearing before Judge Alter proceeded, it was apparent that Dr. Martin' testimony, based upon his psychiatric evaluation of Jimmy, and mine were in direct conflict. I had done some research on hype-reroticism before I was called to testify.

Judge Alter accepted my credentials, extensively cited by the attorney for Jimmy's father, and I was closely examined regarding the test and interview procedures I'd employed, particularly how I interpreted the results, as well as my findings. As soon as I'd concluded and stated that Jimmy seemed unharmed in any way as a result of the alleged incidents, Judge alter said "I'd like to ask a few questions myself".

"I assume you are aware of Dr. Martin' findings and conclusions," she began.

"Yes, I am."

"Well how then would you compare your impressions with his, regarding his view that Jimmy was hyper-eroticized by his experience, i.e. showering with his father and his girlfriend, after having earlier witnessed their having sex together? Dr. Martin, as you know has already testified that Jimmy might have been affected developmentally by this experience."

"Dr. Martin is a highly regarded psychiatrist and the author of several texts on child development," I began. "I therefore have no intention of challenging his conclusion based upon his frame of reference or his experience.

"Well," asked Judge Alter, "are you in agreement with his conclusion or not? It sounds to me like you disagree with his findings."

I turned to face the Judge directly. "Well, Your Honor, I believe Dr. Martin's conclusion is based upon a traditional Freudian or psychoanalytic point of view."

"Well, do you agree or disagree?" Judge Alter asked again. I got the impression that she was growing a bit impatient with me.

"It would be hard to disagree with him within his theoretical context, Your Honor."

"So?"

"But there are other explanations, other points of view, other ways of viewing the subsequent effects of these alleged incidents on Jimmy."

"Go on. I'm listening."

"I would argue, Your Honor, that the hyper-eroticism explanation need not apply in this case, that there may be a simpler view of the significance of Jimmy's experience." I saw a faint smile on Judge Alter's face. I felt enough of a boost to keep going.

"In fact, most kids of five, six and seven tend to drive their teachers and parents a little crazy with constant questions and even fun-making about 'butts', 'pee-pee', 'poop' and sexual parts in general."

Judge Alter laughed, "Yes, and so I've observed."

"So, I think a more parsimonious view of what led Jimmy to do a lot of later questioning about sex was just that, a heightened interest, from a developmental point of view; that is, in a woman s body parts, which he had evidently observed were different from a man's. In other words, his interest was probably simply intensified by his unusual experience, not the cause of abnormal preconceptions over a long period of time as the concept of hyper-eroticism implies, and certainly not resulting in the long-lasting effects attributable to trauma. If, a few years from now, Jimmy's preoccupation with sex and body parts were to persist, yes — then I would go along with the hyper-eroticism viewpoint. But, from my observations, and from the data I have obtained, seven-year-old Jimmy is currently no more sexually preoccupied than most kids his age. I, therefore, must disagree with Dr. Martin. I foresee no later, recurring abnormalities arising from incidents in question.

I watched the judge nodding affirmatively to what I had said. I then outlined some of my test findings, including drawings Jimmy had done, to support my conclusions. It seemed apparent from her continued nodding and facial expression that she had come to agree with my position. I, therefore, kept any further elaboration of my interpretations brief and to the point. I knew that a lengthy cross-examination by the attorney representing Jimmy s mother was soon to follow.

Anyone who has served as an expert witness knows that the job of the opposing attorney during cross-examination, once your credentials have been accepted, and your findings presented, is to try to destroy your credibility and thereby throw doubt on your conclusions. Consequently, there are many specific questions about your actual expertise which might contradict the import of your credentials. There are direct references to your possible bias, your financial gain from the proceedings, and even seemingly insignificant questions about the validity of the methods you employed to arrive at your conclusions. Sometimes, in fact, the line of inquiry frequently pursued by the cross-examiner is important only in that he or she might confuse you, make you contradict yourself, and/or cause you to look inept or even foolish. From the point of view of the expert witness, therefore, the period of cross-examination can be draining. Getting annoyed by it all also has to be controlled lest it affect your appearance of credibility. If you "lose it" in response to the lawyer's questions then as the saying go, you've "lost it!" Your appearance of unswerving objectivity must be maintained no matter what and the lawyers for both sides know that. The lawyer for your side will often seek to protect you in such situations will often seek to protect you in such situations by questioning the relevance of the cross-examiner's efforts to challenge your expertise and the validity of your findings. This case was no different.

When you tested Jimmy what test procedures did you use?" asked Morton Feldstone, the mother's lawyer. So I described the tests and methods I'd used.

"And did you also use a test of visual-motor or eye-hand coordination?" Evidently, a consultant to Feldstone had whispered something to him.

"Yes, I did — but I don't see how my findings from that test had anything to do with my conclusions about Jimmy's present emotional state."

"Please answer my question," said Feldstone, with obvious disdain. "Your Honor, would you please direct the witness to just answer my questions."

"Please respond as you are directed," said the Judge.

"Okay," I replied. I slumped in my seat a little.

"Did you use a test referred to as the Bender-Gestalt Visual-Motor Test?" asked Feldstone.

"Yes, I did, but —"

"Please answer the question, yes or no."

"Yes, I did."

"And why did you use that particular test?"

I explained that I used the Bender routinely and that I was looking to rule out any developmental visual-motor learning disability or perceptual handicap that might negatively affect Jimmy's self-esteem.

"And did you find any such defect or disability affecting his normal development?"

"No, not at all; there was no suggestion of any problem or developmental delay in his eye-hand coordination — ah, I see your point," I added. "You're looking for indications of developmental delay."

"Please stick to simply answering my questions," commented Feldstone, having raised his eyebrows in mock despair so that the Judge might see how difficult a witness I was.

"No, no disabling factors, and nothing suggestive of developmental delay," I reiterated.

"Are you aware that psychologists who use the Bender often describe their findings as objectively as possible, in fact, in terms of what are called Deviation Scores?"

"Yes, I am." Inwardly, I began to smile. Listening to how his line of questioning was developing. I sensed where he was going.

"But you didn't use that method of scoring the Bender, did you?" asked Feldstone.

"No," I answered, "I am familiar with use of deviation scores when interpreting the Bender, but I generally don't use that system."

"Well, then how do you use the Bender?" Feldstone smirked. "Would you please describe your methods, the methods you used, to the Judge?"

"Certainly, I've been trained to employ a more qualitative analysis of a subject's Bender reproductions," I replied. I was now sure what Feldstone was trying to do. He wanted to discredit my examination technique, and thereby my conclusions. My lawyer made a move to object about Feldstone's questions, but I waved him off.

Feldstone continued, "Would it not have been necessary to interpret Jimmy's performance regarding possible developmental delay, as Dr. Martin has suggested, by using a deviation scoring method — you know, to see if Jimmy's copying of the designs truly suggested any more significant developmental visual-motor problem — or delay?"

"No," I quickly answered. "First of all, a slow- developing eye-hand coordination problem is unlike what is meant within the broader concept of developmental delay to which Dr. Martin has alluded. The sort of delay Dr. Martin refers to is much more pervasive. Slow-developing eye-hand control is normally a function of physical maturation. If I'd found any evidence of a more significant delay with Jimmy, I would have then also checked for the other aspects of physical development which might have affected him emotionally, but I found none."

"How about deviation scores?" Feldstone persisted. "How about you're not having used the deviation scores?"

"Thank you for reminding me." I couldn't help a bit of sarcasm. "I don't usually use the deviation score index when evaluating the Bender designs. I have found it to be a superficial way of assessing a subject's copying efforts — almost a distraction, you might say, from doing an overall analysis of the child's performance."

"So, you prefer using your so-called qualitative approach rather than the more objective and standardized scoring method others use for interpretation?"

"Yes, that's correct."

"And, that's because, as you put it, you were trained that way?" Again, Feldstone's eyebrows were arched, this time to convey incredulity.

"Yes, that's correct. That's how I was trained."

"What responsible trainer would teach you to choose a more subjective, qualitative approach over a more objective one?"

"The fact that it's qualitative doesn't mean that it's less accurate — ask any clinician —"

Feldstone interrupted. "Answer the question!" he demanded. "Who trained you to use the test that way?"

"Loretta Bender," I replied. "the *author* of the Bender-Gestalt test."

Feldstone turned ashen. The Judge laughed out loud. The lawyer for our side threw his arms in the air as if we had scored a touchdown.

After a moment or two, having made a lawyer's cardinal error, the fatal mistake of pursuing a line of inquiry without knowing where it might lead, an embarrassed Feldstone simply said . . .

"No more questions, Your Honor."

The proceedings heard before Judge Alter continued for a few more days with several delays in between. Having practically been applauded when I left the stand, I knew my job had been successfully accomplished. I had given the Judge a viable, alternative explanation of Jimmy's behavior to counter Martin's hyper-eroticism theory, and I had made the cross-examining attorney appear foolish in the Judge's eyes. The rest of the case went smoothly. There was little further evidence offered to support the plaintiff's presentation that Jimmy had been damaged by his father's sexual involvement with his girlfriend. Jimmy's advocate, in fact, had also advised the Judge that he'd uncovered no evidence to suggest anything detrimental in Jimmy's current relationship with his father. In fact, he told the Judge that he agreed with what my observation that Jimmy very much missed his visitations with his father.

In retrospect, I believe that there was damage done because of the need to involve Jimmy in all the legal proceedings, proceedings which further alienated his parents and which confused him about why he'd had to be kept from seeing his father. Two weeks later, the Judge handed down her decision. She dismissed all charges against Jimmy's father as having been unsubstantiated by fact. She removed all visitation constraints and apologized for any harmful effects that may have occurred as a result of the visitation restraints.

Approximately a year passed before I heard again from Jimmy's father. He reported that Jimmy was doing well in school, and had pretty much gotten over the stresses created by the lawsuit. He thanked me again for my court appearance and my testimony.

Despite Jimmy's father's having won the suit brought against him by his ex-wife, I was troubled by the judicial system's way of handling such matters. I felt that Jimmy had been exposed to an inordinate amount of stress which might have been avoided through pre-hearing mediation regarding the underlying issues between Jimmy's mother and father. I have seen many similar cases and in every instance, in my opinion, it is the child who suffers most. At least Jimmy didn't show signs of having been hurt by the legal maneuvers which disrupted his life. But, after all, Martin may have been right about some long-term impact on Jimmy, not because of the kind of hyper-eroticism he professed concern about, but because of how our system of justice doesn't always serve what may really be in a child's best interests.

ENDNOTE: FROM THE AUTHOR'S WIFE

It has given me great pleasure to serve as the editor for my husband's memoirs. I am extremely proud of his work, especially because, both during his active working years and for many years after his retirement, I was often approached by strangers who, on hearing my name, would come up and say, "Your husband rescued my marriage," or "Your husband helped my child so much," or "Your husband saved my life!"

Printed in the United States
by Baker & Taylor Publisher Services